# PERSONAL DISCIPLESHIP

*Holy Spirit Top Level*

# PERSONAL DISCIPLESHIP

## *Holy Spirit Top Level*

# BENJAMIN MAIRA

authorHOUSE®

*AuthorHouse™ UK Ltd.*
*500 Avebury Boulevard*
*Central Milton Keynes, MK9 2BE*
*www.authorhouse.co.uk*
*Phone: 08001974150*

*Ministry Edition*

*Published by AuthorHouse 5/7/2013*

*ISBN: 978-1-4817-9451-0 (sc)*
*ISBN: 978-1-4817-9452-7 (e)*

*All quotations of the Holy Bible are taken from Authorized King James version Copyright © 1989 Thomas Nelson, Inc*

*Any people depicted in stock imagery provided by Thinkstock are models, and such images are being used for illustrative purposes only. Certain stock imagery © Thinkstock.*

*This book is printed on acid-free paper.*

*My website www.sentone.org.uk*

# ACKNOWLEDGEMENTS

Thanks to the outstanding ministers of the Lord whose ministry gave me Holy Spirit discipleship and impartation upon my life during my early days of Christianity, their input to my relationship with God was very good and edifying.

Special thanks to my wife Flora and the children (Benson, Boniface and Barry) for their love, support and diligence. I know it was difficult to do two things at the same time (loving and caring for you with labouring in writing this book) but through the Lord's help we made it. Let us give all the glory to Jesus Christ.

# DEDICATION

To all people of the world, readers and the Lord Jesus Christ

To all people on planet earth, this book is my labour in the gospel and work of the Lord. It is the Lord's desire that you know personal discipleship, and so it is mine too. May the Lord give you understanding on what discipleship is all about. From today, become a devoted disciple of the Lord Jesus Christ. This book is my doing part of what I love dearly: *world apostleship and discipleship* to you and all the people around you.

To the readers, since I knew the word discipleship, I have for long time desire to write and place this book in your hands. This book is for you.

Above all I dedicate this book to the Lord Jesus Christ our Saviour; you have made me the minister of the gospel and work of the Lord. I have come to know personal discipleship is of God.

# PROLOGUE

## Discipleship in action

Jesus Christ began his ministry after baptism by John the Baptist at the river Jordan. Jordan is a place of the Holy Spirit coming upon the Lord. The Holy Spirit anointed Jesus Christ at the River Jordan. Jesus Christ was born at Bethlehem. He fled to Egypt (a place of rescue and refuge). Jesus Christ grew up at Nazareth. The ministry centre of Jesus Christ was Galilee and the Lord died and rose in Jerusalem.

Before the Holy Spirit came upon Jesus Christ (Luke 3:21-23) there was no ministry, no message, no miracles, no multitudes and no mentorship. But when the Holy Spirit came upon Jesus Christ all things changed in the country of Israel. It was the Holy Spirit who empower Jesus Christ to do his work and apostleship in Israel. In his work and apostleship Jesus Christ touched the poor, the sick and the sinners. In the words of Scriptures, Luke 4:18-19 says:

*The Spirit of the Lord is upon me, because he hath anointed me to preach the gospel to the poor; he hath sent me to heal the brokenhearted, to preach deliverance to the captives, and recovering of sight to the blind, to set at* liberty *them that are bruised, to preach the acceptable year of the Lord.*

Also Luke 5:31-32 says:

*And Jesus answering said unto them, they that are whole need not a physician; but they that are sick. I came not to call the righteous, but sinners to repentance.*

Although Jesus Christ preached the gospel to the poor, healed the sick and called sinners to repentance but his ministry and apostleship had another gracious and glorious thing: discipleship. After Luke chapter 3,4 and 5 the ministry and apostleship of the Lord grew and increased to the highest level when Jesus Christ had multitudes of disciples in Luke 6,7,14 and 19. Jesus Christ was successful in both *apostleship and discipleship.* Jesus Christ came to preach the gospel and do the work of the Lord but also to make new disciples in Israel and worldwide. We see discipleship results in the book of Acts also. By the time Jesus Christ went to heaven, he left hundred and twenty disciples. But when the Holy Spirit came on upper room, three thousand souls were saved. Then after the miracle of the lame five thousand souls were added unto the Lord. Then Acts chapter 6,9,13 to14 and 16 to19 show that the disciples of the Lord grew in multitudes and multiplied in number. And today more than ever we need *discipleship in action.* We need people to find the Lord and follow him in large number. The book of Luke and Acts is about discipleship in action.

And finally in our days, ministry and church is about discipleship in action. The Lord wants his ministry and church to grow and increase both spiritually and numerically.

The Lord Jesus Christ desires for us is to make many new disciples not few. Discipleship in action is not only for Israel but the whole world. The Lord intends that discipleship in action to happen in global scale dimension. Are you a disciple of the Lord? Became one today! Are you making new disciples? Please, do it today for the Lord. I exhort you in the Lord, to read the book of Luke and Acts and experience discipleship in action.

BENJAMIN MAIRA

# INTRODUCTION

## The call of discipleship

The ministry and apostleship of Jesus Christ was not only about the gospel with signs and wonders. The Lord Jesus Christ truly preached the gospel and performed many signs and wonders but he also did discipleship. The Lord Jesus Christ called the twelve disciples and made great multitude of disciples. The twelve disciples he called them one by one. But the multitudes of the disciples, Jesus Christ called them in large number through his public crusades in Israel and the cities around. The multitudes of disciples found the Lord and followed him, as Jesus Christ preached the gospel with signs and wonders. In the words of Scripture, Luke 5:15 says:

*But so much the more went there a fame abroad of him: and great multitudes came together to hear, and to be healed by him of their infirmities*

We see also the Lord Jesus Christ called the twelve disciples individually. Jesus Christ called Matthew alone. Jesus Christ found Matthew and told him, follow me. And Matthew followed him. Now that is the call of discipleship. The call of discipleship is to follow the Lord. In the words of Scripture, Luke 5:27-28 says:

*And after these things he went forth, and saw a publican, named Levi, sitting at the receipt of custom: and he said unto him, Follow me. And he left all, rose up, and followed him*

Today, the Lord Jesus Christ is calling you not only to find the Lord but more importantly to follow him. How do you follow the Lord? You follow the Lord by the Holy Spirit, his power and voice of God. The Holy Spirit has come to empower you to be a disciple of the Lord. In Luke 24:49 and Acts 1:8, Jesus Christ spoke of the power of God and the Holy Spirit. In John 10:27, Jesus Christ spoke of his divine voice, which the disciples needed to hear. You cannot be a disciple of the Lord without the Holy Spirit, power and the voice of God. Why the voice of God? The Holy Spirit speaks to disciples. The Holy Spirit empowers disciples and the Holy Spirit lives inside the disciples of the Lord. The Lord Jesus Christ put great emphasis on the Holy Spirit, power and voice of God. And before Jesus Christ went to heaven, he took time to teach on the Holy Spirit, power and voice of God. A successful disciple of the Lord must receive the Holy Spirit, power and hear God's voice. The disciples of the Lord in the book of Acts were successful because they knew and experienced the Holy Spirit, power and voice of God.

As you read my book, *Personal Discipleship*, **ask the Holy Spirit to teach you and impart to you** special instructions for discipleship. Read and obtain life input for you.

# TABLE OF CONTENTS

# CHAPTER 1
## *Discipleship Today*

## Modern disciples

Then departed Barnabas to Tarsus, for to seek Saul: and when he had found him, he brought him unto Antioch. And it came to pass, that a whole year they assembled themselves with the church, and taught much people. And the disciples were called Christians first in Antioch

**Acts 11:25-26**

## What is discipleship?

Disciples were first called Christians! What does that mean? It means disciples were identified with the Lord Jesus Christ. Christians are people belong to Christ. Or people who have Christ likeness. It is like in Acts 4:13, when they saw the boldness of Peter and John, and perceived they were unlearned and ignorant they took the knowledge of them that they had been with Jesus. What made difference in Peter and John was Jesus' discipleship in their life. In other words it was the teaching of Jesus Christ and the Holy Spirit touch. And here at the Antioch church the disciples were transformed because of the teaching of the word of God and the Holy Spirit touch. Barnabas and Paul taught much people in the church for the whole year. Discipleship makes impact. And thus is why discipleship is very important to people today. If we are going to impact the world today we need discipleship. In his ministry and apostleship, Jesus did also discipleship. The apostles, all of them were involved in the gospel and work of the Lord but also in discipleship. Discipleship does not only mean training for ministry. Discipleship has deeper meaning than that. Even in Jesus time, discipleship was not limited to training for ministry but also discipleship meant to find Christ the Lord and follow him. Or discipleship was meant the call of Christ to know him and follow him. Discipleship is a life of dedication. Discipleship is lifetime devotion to the Lord Jesus Christ. Discipleship is not three years commitment to a school of ministry until you graduate for ministry. Discipleship and Christianity goes together, hand in hand. Who is a disciple? A disciple is a devoted Christian. A disciple is a saved person. Notice, these disciples who were first called Christians, in Acts 11:19-21 they turn to the Lord after the preaching of the Name of Jesus and the word of God when the hand of the Lord (the Spirit) was with people who preached to them. Discipleship is not just training for ministry; it is first believing and turning to the Lord. Then teaching of new disciples can be made. Understand salvation is new creation. A dead spirit must be recreated and made new before teaching, nurturing and maturing of a person.

The term Christian or Christianity is widely used today. And the term discipleship is misused today. People take discipleship as some sort of training and stop there. Apart from the twelve disciples in the book of Luke 6,7,14 and 19, there were other Disciples of Christ in a spiritual meaning not just training for ministry even if you are not saved! A disciple is first and foremost a saved person, not just a student. A disciple is an adherent to the Lord Jesus Christ faith and the gospel of God. In the book of Acts, all the disciples from Acts 2, 4, 6,9,11,13 to14,16 to19,20 to 21 and so on, were all first saved. Before the coming of the Holy Spirit and power of God, discipleship was partly training for ministry and following Christ for salvation. But after the coming of the Holy Spirit and his power, discipleship first means to receive the gift of salvation then training. You cannot train a sinner, a sinner need preaching of the gospel of salvation. Preaching is inspirational and impactful. Teaching is instructional and imparting of truth. When Jesus said in Matthew 28:19-20 go make disciples of all nations, he meant call people to believe in him and turn to the Lord. Make disciples means someone who is not to be made a believer in the Lord. If you look carefully, the word to teach is twice used, firstly it means to make disciples and then to teach them to observe all the things of the Lord, as I have commanded you, the Lord said.

## The seven meaning of discipleship

Luke 5:27 shows clearly discipleship is a call of Christ to follow him. The Lord Jesus Christ appeared to Matthew and said to him, "follow me". Discipleship means to find Christ and follow him. To the church at Corinth, Paul once said these words: *be ye followers of me, even as I also am of Christ.* John had disciples but it was Jesus Christ who took the term discipleship to the next level. In his ministry and apostleship to Israel, Jesus Christ did not mean that discipleship was limited to training for ministry. Discipleship is also adherence to the Lord's faith. A disciple has personal relationship with his Lord and Master. The seven meaning of discipleship are:

1.  Adherence to the Master and Lord's faith. A disciple is a believer, one who has turned to the Lord's faith and the gospel of God.

2.  To find and follow the Lord. A disciple is a person who has received Jesus Christ as Lord and Saviour. A disciple is saved person. Discipleship is the call of Christ to know him and follow him.

3.  To learn and do the word of God. A disciple is a learner and doer of the word of God. A disciple is dedicated to the teaching of his Master and Lord Jesus Christ.

4.  Devotion to the Lord. A disciple is a devoted Christian. A disciple knows Christ. A disciple has Christ likeness and belongs to Christ the Lord.

5.  The making of new disciples. Discipleship is first making new disciples (sinners first saved) then teaching them to observe all the commandments of the Lord.

6.  Preparation and training for apostleship. Preparation and training are important for the gospel and work of the Lord.

7.  To teach other people to observe the

commandments of the Lord after salvation. Discipleship is nurturing and maturing people by the word of God and the Holy Spirit.

## The characteristics of a disciple

A disciple has unique characteristics. The characteristics of a disciple are found in the book of Luke and Acts. The Lord Jesus Christ taught some of the characteristics of a disciple. The Lord said: a disciple abide in the word, a disciple prays, a disciple follow him, a disciple is devoted to him, a disciple imitates him and a disciple is not greater than his Master and Lord. One of the greatest characteristics of a disciple is to make new disciples. The Lord Jesus Christ said to his twelve apostles: *go into all nations and make disciples*. To a disciple, Jesus Christ is not only the Master, Lord and Teacher but also role model and living example. The Lord Jesus Christ came on earth, to show us an example that any person can obey the gospel and know God. If Jesus Christ obeyed and followed God and his word, then all people can do the same thing and more. Jesus Christ was a disciple of God! Why? Because Jesus Christ said, whatever I do, I see the Father do. The Father is still working, and the Son also is working now. The characteristics of a disciple will enable you to be a good disciple. The characteristics of a disciple are:

1. **A disciple is saved (faith in Christ)**
2. **A disciple is filled with joy and the Holy Spirit**
3. **A disciple is called, anointed and used by Holy Spirit (used for service)**

4.  **A disciple has dynamic ministry (anointed ministry)**

5.  **A disciple serve the people of God with good works**

6.  **A disciple makes new disciples**

7.  **A disciple deliver the captives**

8.  **A disciple serve God and minister in the Holy Spirit**

9.  **A disciple serve God and minister the gospel**

10.  **A disciple demonstrates love**

11.  **A disciple bear fruit**

12.  **A disciple abide in the word**

13.  **A disciple is a devoted Christian to the Lord**

14.  **A disciple carry his own cross and follow the Lord**

15.  **A disciple do not backslide**

16.  **A disciple imitate his Master and Lord Jesus Christ**

17.  **A disciple has a local church and sound minister (pastor)**

18.  **A disciple receive preparation and training (he is teachable)**

19.  **A disciple is reported well**

20.  **A disciple is chosen with good report, the Holy Spirit and wisdom**

21. **A disciple minister to the poor (meet a need with seed)**

22. **A disciple minister to the sick (healing of others)**

23. **A disciple minister to the sinners (salvation of others)**

24. **A disciple is not greater than his Master and Lord Jesus Christ but is like Him**

25. **A disciple is a person of hospitality and giving**

26. **A disciple is devoted to prayer, the Holy Spirit and the word of God**

## Salvation, the Holy Spirit and ministry

But the Lord said to him, "Go, for he is a chosen vessel of mine to bear my name before Gentiles, kings, and the children of Israel. For I will show him how many things he must suffer for My name's sake."And Ananias went his way and entered the house; and laying his hands on him he said, "Brother Saul, the Lord Jesus, who appeared to you on the road as you came, has sent me that you may receive your sight and be filled with the Holy Spirit." Immediately there fell from his eyes *something* like scales, and he received his sight at once; and he arose and was baptized. So when he had received food, he was strengthened. Then Saul spent some days with the disciples at Damascus.

**Acts 9:15-19**

What are three gifts of God to a new disciple? The answer

is *salvation, the Holy Spirit and ministry*. To the apostle Paul all three gifts of God were done in his life. Paul was saved, filled with the Holy Spirit and called to the ministry after he saw the Lord. In the Scripture above, I want you to see certain words: baptised and then spent some days with disciples, the Holy Spirit and chosen vessel. The three precious gifts of God to Paul were confirmed in one single day. Paul knew there and then, that he has salvation, the Holy Spirit and ministry. *Firstly,* Ananias said Brother Saul, that means he was saved and he is among the brethren in the Lord Jesus Christ. Another fact about salvation is the statement: baptized and spent some days with the disciples, that means Paul was saved and became a new disciple in the Lord Jesus Christ. *Secondly,* Ananias said, the Lord Jesus has sent me that you may receive your sight and be filled with the Holy Spirit, that means on that day Paul receive the Holy Spirit and his touch. *Thirdly*, I love what I am about to say. I don't know about you! It is this statement: But the Lord said to him, *"Go, for he is a chosen vessel of mine to bear my name before Gentiles, kings, and the children of Israel. Those words of the Lord are about ministry. What a gracious and glorious day to a new disciple. In one day, the Lord used Ananias to confirm salvation, the Holy Spirit and ministry to a new disciple.* To you it might be salvation, the Holy Spirit and ministry did not happen one day, but you must know as a disciple you have the most three precious gifts of God. The right order of God is salvation, the Holy Spirit and ministry. Not another way round. First is salvation, second is the Holy Spirit and third is ministry. Not ministry, Holy Spirit and finally salvation. And not even the Holy Spirit, salvation and lastly ministry. The correct order of the precious gifts of God is *salvation, the Holy Spirit and ministry.* The Holy Spirit is given to a disciple not a sinner or the lost. You must first be a disciple of the Lord Jesus Christ. Thus is why, the Lord Jesus Christ appeared to Paul first before he was filled with the Holy Spirit and his call to the ministry was confirmed by the devoted disciple and a prophet of the Lord, Ananias. A disciple must be saved first, then receive the Holy Spirit and ministry. Consider the words of Scripture in John 7:37-39, we read:

*On the last day, that great day of the feast, Jesus stood and cried out, saying, "If anyone thirsts, let him come to Me and drink. He who believes in Me, as the Scripture has said, out of his heart will* flow rivers *of living water."But this He spoke concerning the* Spirit, *whom those believing in Him would receive; for the Holy Spirit was not yet given, because Jesus was not yet glorified.*

Believe has to do with salvation. Believe has to do with first call upon the name of the Lord Jesus Christ for salvation (the prayer of salvation). Then you receive the Holy Spirit. Salvation comes first then followed by the Holy Spirit. In John 14:6,12, verse 6 is salvation (I am the way, the truth and life, no man comes to my Father but by me) and verse twelve is ministry (he who believe in me, the works that I do he shall do also). Salvation comes first then followed by ministry. If you put together John 7:37-39 and John 14:6,12, the word believe should be first, then the Holy Spirit and ministry. And that means we have what already discussed salvation, the Holy Spirit and ministry.

## How to grow in personal discipleship

To be a new disciple of the Lord Jesus Christ is a gracious and glorious thing. To be a new disciple of the Lord Jesus Christ is a lifetime journey. Personal discipleship is a new life commitment. Personal discipleship is not start and stop thing. You have believed the Lord Jesus Christ, then you need to follow him daily, be nurtured and mature in the Lord. Personal discipleship is a daily walk with the Lord as you pursue his purpose and grace in your life. In Luke 14:25-27, the Lord said these words:

*And there went great multitudes with him: and he turned, and said unto them, If any man come to me, and hate not his father, and* mother, *and wife, and children, and brethren, and sisters, yea, and his own life also, he cannot be my disciple. And whosoever doth not bear his cross, and come after me, cannot be my disciple.*

**Luke 14:25-27**

The Lord said to the multitudes three things: firstly, put Jesus Christ first than all people (see, verse 26) Secondly, be ready to obey the gospel and follow Jesus Christ daily, and to suffer for his sake and the gospel's even if it means martyrdom (see verse 27). In verse 33, the Lord said the third thing: make a total life commitment for the Lord and leave all things. Leave all selfish interests. Do you want to grow in personal discipleship? Then you must seek and follow the Lord Jesus Christ on daily basis. As a new disciple you need to grow in:

1.  <u>Salvation</u>: you need to know what has happened to you. Your identity, rights and privilege in salvation of the Lord. You need to know how to live in your new salvation. You need to be nurtured and matured in your salvation.

2.  <u>The Holy Spirit</u>: you need to know more the person and work of the Holy Spirit. You are the temple of the Holy Spirit. The Holy Spirit has sealed you; he is guarantee of your eternal salvation. The Holy Spirit renews you. The Holy Spirit dwells in you. The Holy Spirit fills and leads you to the things of the Lord.

3.  <u>The Anointing</u>: you need the power of God. Personal discipleship is possible through the power of God. Each day seek the Lord and his power. You need fresh power for each new day. Yesterday anointing is not enough for today. The anointing is for salvation and ministry. Ask the Holy Spirit to anoint you with his power.

4.  <u>Devotions</u>: devotions means spend time in the presence of God. How do you do daily devotions? You do daily devotions though prayer and the word of God. Learn to talk to God daily and read the Holy Bible, God will speak to you. Devote yourself to the Lord, prayer and the word of God.

5.  <u>Witnessing</u>: the task of a disciple is to make new disciples. So tell others what God has done to you. Tell other people about the goodness of the Lord. Testify the gospel and work of the Lord in

your life. Share with other your joy of salvation. A disciple is a witness of Jesus Christ.

6. <u>Local church</u>: a disciple needs a local church. A local church is a church of one place. A disciple needs to have relationship with the Lord and fellow disciples. A disciple must be committed to a local church. A local church enables and enhances you in personal discipleship.

7. <u>Pastoral ministry</u>: a disciple needs pastoral ministry. A pastor is a leader, shepherd and sound minister who will nurture and mature you. A pastor is a special ministry gift of the Lord to you. A pastor edifies you, exhort you and equip you to serve God and do the work of the ministry.

## Discipleship and Christianity

Then Agrippa said to Paul, "You almost persuade me to become a Christian."And Paul said, "I would to God that not only you, but also all who hear me today, might become both almost and altogether such as I am, except for these chains."

**Acts 26:28-29**

## What is Christianity?

Christianity is referred to many as a religion. But Christianity is more than a religion. Christianity can be defined as a personal relationship with the Lord Jesus Christ. Christianity happens when a person receive Jesus Christ as

Lord and Saviour. The term Christianity comes from the word Christian. The word Christian is found three times in the Holy Bible. *The first time*: the word Christian is found in Acts 11:26. The Scripture says, the disciples were first called in Antioch. The reason why the disciples were first called Christians it was because the disciples were like Christ in behaviour, deed and speech. *The second time*: the word Christian is found in Acts 26:28-29. The Scripture says, Agrippa said to Paul; almost persuade me to be a Christian. And Paul replied emphasizing he is a Christian and he prayed God all people were like him except these bonds. The third time: the word Christian is found in 1 Peter 4:16. The Scripture says, *yet if any man suffer as a Christian, let him not be ashamed; but let him glorify God on this behalf.* Peter spoke about the importance of a person to suffer as a Christian without shame and glorify God. Christianity is all about faith in Christ. Christianity is not just a religion or denomination. Religion is about man seeking God. But Christianity is about God seeking the lost man. In the words of Scripture, Acts 24:23-25 says:

*And he commanded a centurion to keep Paul, and to let him have* liberty, *and that he should forbid none of his acquaintance to minister or come unto him. And after certain days, when Felix came with his wife Drusilla, which was a Jewess, he sent for Paul, and heard him concerning the faith in Christ. And as he reasoned of righteousness, temperance, and judgment to come, Felix trembled, and answered, Go thy way for this time; when I have a convenient season, I will call for thee.*

Christianity being faith in Christ deals with three main things: righteousness, temperance and judgement to come.

Let me explain these three things, as Paul did. *Righteousness*: faith in Christ gives you righteousness. When you believe Christ, God count you a righteous person as though you never sinned. Christianity is righteousness by faith not works. Romans 1:16-17 says: *For I am not ashamed of the* gospel of Christ*: for it is the power of God unto salvation to everyone that believeth; to the Jew first, and also to the Greek. For therein is the righteousness of God revealed from faith to faith: as it is written, The just shall live by faith.* Christianity is based on the finished work of Christ (the Cross) and his resurrection power. Christianity is about the death, the burial and resurrection of the Lord Jesus Christ. Most world religions are established upon the life of the founder not so with Christianity. Christianity is about the crucifixion, burial and resurrection of the Christ.

*Temperance*: temperance is self control. The word temperance is found three times in Acts 24:25, Galatians 5:22-23 and 2 Peter 1:6. God expects a Christian to live in self-control. In Galatians 5:22-23, self-control is one of the nine flavours of the fruit of the Spirit. When you become a Christian (saved person), you receive the Holy Spirit and his presence. The Holy Spirit and his presence produce self-control. In 2 Peter 1:6, the apostle Peter said to your knowledge add self-control. Christianity is a new life of self control and put on the Lord Jesus Christ all the time here on earth. Romans 11:13-14 says: *let us walk honestly, as in the day; not in rioting and drunkenness, not in chambering and wantonness, not in strife and envying. But put ye on the Lord Jesus Christ, and make not provision for the flesh, to fulfil the lusts thereof.* Put on the Lord Jesus Christ that means to be clothed with him.

The Christ of Christianity gives the new life of self-control and sound mind.

*Judgement to come:* God is Lord, Father and Judge. The days are coming you will see God face to face not only as Lord and Father but also Judge. One day according to the Holy Bible, God will judge the world. Acts 17:30-31 says these words: *and the times of this* ignorance God *winked at; but now commandeth all* men *everywhere to repent: because he hath appointed a day, in the which he will judge the world in righteousness by that man whom he hath ordained; whereof he hath given assurance unto all men, in that he hath raised him from the dead.* There is such a thing as "the judgement day of God". In Romans 2:16, Paul the apostle said, in the day, God shall judge all the secrets of men by Jesus Christ according to my gospel. The day of Judgement is coming! Are you prepared to see God? In 2 Corinthians 5:9-10, Paul the apostle wrote these words: *wherefore we labour, that, whether present or absent, we may be accepted of him. For we must all appear before the judgment* seat of Christ*; that every one may receive the things done in his body, according to that he hath done, whether it be good or bad.* The judgement seat of Christ! It is true. You will be called by name and stand before the judgement seat of Christ, and give account of your life on earth. Like God, Jesus Christ is Lord, Saviour and Judge. The Scripture says that, God has committed all judgement to the Son.

## The power and authority of a disciple

Then he called his twelve disciples together, and gave them

power and authority over all devils, and to cure diseases. And he sent them to preach the kingdom of God, and to heal the sick.

**Luke 9:1-2**

God has given every disciple power and authority in the New Testament. When God created Adam and Eve he gave them dominion (Genesis 1:26). The Psalmist also declares of this great authority that God gave to Adam and Eve (Psalms 8:4-6). God crowned his people with his power and authority. Unfortunately by sinning against God, Adam and Eve lost their power and authority. God sent the Lord Jesus Christ to restore all Adam and Eve lost and so much more. The Lord Jesus Christ has done more and gave power and authority to every disciple and Christian. The authority of a disciple is also known as *kingdom authority, believers' authority or spiritual authority.* **What is authority**? Authority is the right to act or to exercise or to govern. You have the right to exercise the power of God over Satan, sin and sickness or anything that is contrary to the word of God. You have authority to rebuke it. **What is rebuke**? To rebuke a thing is to speak to it, stop that is enough! To rebuke a thing, means also to say something opposite the current situation. Authority is the key to open and close (Matthew 16:19). If you have a key you can open and close the door. Every disciple has been given keys of the kingdom to bind and loose. To bind and loose you also do so by the power of God or the anointing. That is why when Jesus sent his disciples to speak the gospel and minister healing to the sick, and he gave them power and authority. **What is power?** Power is ability of God or the anointing for service. Authority consists of the name of the Lord Jesus Christ (Luke 9:49-50), the word of God (Luke 7:7-8), the power of the Holy Spirit (Luke 24:49). There are two types of authority: the authority of a minister and authority of a Christian or disciple. The authority of a minister is the highest level operation. When I say a minister I refer to sound ministers of the gospel listed in Ephesians 4:11, namely apostles, prophets, evangelists, pastors and teachers. A minister of the gospel speak with great authority because of the ministry gift he or she has, they are called, empowered and sent by the Holy Spirit, to serve God and minister to people by grace. If a Christian or disciple uses properly God given authority and power he cannot faint, fail or fall. Authority and power of God is given to you for total success in life and service. Luke 10:19 says these words: *Behold, I give unto you power to tread on serpents and scorpions, and over all the power of the enemy: and nothing shall by any means hurt you.*

## Discipleship in the New Testament

Discipleship is the New Testament thing. There is little to say in Old Testament about discipleship or disciples. The word disciple is found in Isaiah 8:16. God said to Isaiah these words: *bind up the testimony, seal the law among my disciples.* The disciples in Isaiah time could have been the Lord's people. For Isaiah 8:18 says: I and the children who the Lord has given me are for signs and wonders in Israel. Israel is the Lord's people. Then there is Moses, Samuel and Elijah who had disciples. Joshua was a disciple of Moses. Elisha was a disciple of Elijah. And both Samuel and Elijah had a school of prophets, and the disciples were called sons of the prophets. Hence, we can conclude discipleship is the New Testament thing. In other words discipleship belongs more to the New Testament than the Old Testament. Of course, there are things to learn from the Old Testament and follow them as part of the word of God. Discipleship is real thing. Discipleship is of the Lord. In New Testament both John the Baptist and the Lord Jesus Christ had disciples. I am not talking about only the twelve disciples and the seventy disciples, but I am talking about both John and Jesus had multitudes disciples and secret disciples in Israel.

Speaking of Jesus, Luke 7:11 says: *and it came to pass the day after, that he went into a city called Nain; and many of his disciples went with him, and much people.*

Listen to the scripture, it says: and many of his disciples went with him and much people. The Lord Jesus had so many disciples and much people followed him, than the twelve disciples and the seventy disciples. The twelve disciples and the seventy disciples were called and set apart for the gospel and work of the Lord (apostleship). But the multitudes of disciples of Jesus were believers in the Lord. Please, do away with the understanding that Jesus' disciples were the twelve and the seventy disciples and all the multitudes of souls were sinners and the lost. In Jesus' time, there were two groups of multitudes of people: the lost and found. There were multitudes of people who were sinners and multitudes of people who were disciples.

Both in the book of Luke and Acts there is "disciple reference". In the book of Luke, multitudes of disciples are found in Luke 6,7,14 and 19. In the book of acts multitude of disciples are found in Acts 6,9,11,14,17,18,19 and 20. In the book of Acts we see hundred and twenty disciples in Acts chapter one. But then after the Holy Spirit came, the apostles had multitude of disciples such as three thousand were saved in a day (chapter two), five thousand were save (chapter three and four). Then in chapter four, five and six because of the Holy Spirit, power and the gospel there were growth and expansion to the number of disciples in Israel. And today, more than ever in 21st century and modern culture we need growth and expansion of multitudes of disciples. Discipleship and apostleship has not changed, it is still there. And because we have the same Holy Spirit, power and the gospel we can achieve the greatest goal of all: *the multitudes of disciples*. The Lord Jesus and apostles achieved this greatest goal; we too with God on our side can achieve the greatest goal of all. What is the greatest goal of all? The greatest goal of all is to be a disciple and make more and more new disciples by the Holy Spirit, power and the gospel. We all have goals in life and service, but this goal I am talking about is the greatest goal of all. This goal is not a goal of man but the goal of God. If you can achieve your human goals, surely you can achieve the divine goal on planet earth.

# CHAPTER 2
## Discipleship and Impartation

### Impartation for disciples

As they ministered to the Lord, and fasted, the Holy Ghost said, Separate me Barnabas and Saul for the work whereunto I have called them. And when they had fasted and prayed, and laid their hands on them, they sent them away.

**Acts 13:2-3**

Barnabas received his discipleship from Peter and the eleven disciples in Jerusalem. In other words Barnabas became a disciple because of the gospel and the work of the Lord of the apostles in Jerusalem city. Barnabas was saved and received the Holy Spirit in Jerusalem. He became a minister of the gospel under the apostles and the Holy Spirit. It was Barnabas who took Paul and introduced him to the apostles and the church of Jerusalem city. This was when Paul was saved, and the apostles and the brethren did not believe he was a disciple. But Paul was a disciple he met the Lord on the road to Damascus (Acts 9:26-28). Paul was saved and then received the Holy Spirit on the street called straight. The Lord Jesus Christ used a disciple called Ananias to heal

Paul's blindness and lay hands upon him to receive the Holy Spirit. And Paul was healed, strengthened and received the Holy Spirit. This is how Paul and Barnabas became disciples. Paul and Barnabas were saved in different time and places but the Lord brought them together for world apostleship. But before world apostleship Barnabas trained and cared for Paul in the church of the Lord until the day the Holy Spirit sent them away for world apostleship. There are three key words you need to understand: *discipleship, impartation and apostleship.* Barnabas and Paul were first made disciples, then received impartation and sent away for the greatest work of all: apostleship. In the Scripture above, when all ministers sought the Holy Spirit and ministered to the Lord, we see three things call, impartation and send. When other ministers laid their hands on Barnabas and Paul that was *impartation.* What impartation? It is the impartation of grace and power for service. Or in others words it was the impartation of the anointing. We know this from Paul's Epistle to the Romans. In Romans 15:15-19, Paul said he was made a minister of Jesus Christ by grace and he did signs and wonders by the power of the Spirit of God. Where did he receive grace and power? He received grace and power from impartation service at the Antioch church. To be a disciple you need special impartation of grace and power. In the words of Scripture, the Scripture says:

*Nevertheless, brethren, I have written the more boldly unto you in some sort, as putting you in mind, because of the grace that is given to me of* God, *That I should be the minister of Jesus* Christ *to the Gentiles, ministering the gospel of God, that the offering up of the Gentiles might be acceptable, being sanctified by the Holy Ghost. I have therefore whereof I may glory through*

*Jesus Christ in those things which pertain to God. For I will not dare to speak of any of those things which Christ hath not wrought by me, to make the Gentiles obedient, by word and deed, Through mighty signs and wonders, by the power of the Spirit of God; so that from Jerusalem, and round about unto Illyricum, I have fully preached the gospel of Christ*

Also in the book of Ephesus 3:5-7, Paul wrote about grace and power. Paul said he was made a minister of the gospel by the gift of God's grace according to the effectual working of his power. A disciple cannot do world apostleship or the gospel and work of the Lord without grace and power. You need God's impartation upon you. You need grace and power for what God has called you to be and do. In the words of Scripture, the Scripture says:

*Which in other ages was not made known unto the sons of men, as it is now revealed unto his holy apostles and prophets by the Spirit; That the Gentiles should be fellowheirs, and of the same body, and partakers of his promise in Christ by the gospel: Whereof I was made a minister, according to the gift of the grace of God given unto me by the effectual working of his power.*

## Disciples' reference part one

From the book of Luke we find disciples' reference. Disciples' reference has points to help you in life. This disciples' reference is not about only the twelve disciples but all the company of disciples, Jesus had in all of Israel. Disciples' reference starts from Luke five to Luke nineteen with twenty four points. The disciples' reference is as follows:

1.  Luke 5:27, a disciple receive the call to follow the Lord

2.  Luke 6:12-13, the twelve disciples had dual call: discipleship and apostleship

3.  Luke 6:17, the company of disciples hear the Lord

4.  Luke 6:20, disciples are blessed with the kingdom of God

5.  Luke 6:40, a disciple is like his Lord not above him

6.  Luke 7:11, disciples grow in number

7.  Luke 8:9, disciples find answers from the Lord

8.  Luke 8:22, disciples follow instructions

9.  Luke 9:1-2, disciples receive impartation

10. Luke 9:16, disciples serve the people of God

11. Luke 9:18-19, disciples know Jesus is the Christ of God

12. Luke 9:39-41, disciples must have faith to heal the sick

13. Luke 9:53-55, disciples should pray according to the will of the Lord

14. Luke 10:23-24, disciples are blessed with fresh move of God

15. Luke 11:1, disciples should learn to pray

16. Luke 12:1, disciples should watch out

17. Luke 13:22-23, disciples desire salvation of others

18. Luke 14:25-27, disciples should bear their cross daily (the cost of discipleship)

19. Luke 14:33, disciples should live all things for Christ

20. Luke 16:1-2, disciples learn and apply financial stewardship

21. Luke 17:1-3, disciples do well

22. Luke 17:22, disciples hear prophecy and prepare

23. Luke 18:15, disciples should give good treatment not harsh rebuke

24. Luke 19:36-38, disciples praise and worship God for the things he has done

## Discipleship and the Anointing

What is the anointing?

How God anointed Jesus of Nazareth with the Holy Ghost and with power: who went about doing good, and healing all that were oppressed of the devil; for God was with him

**Acts 10:38**

The Lord is called Jesus because he is the Saviour. The Lord he is called Christ because he is anointed with the Holy Spirit and power by God. Who anointed Jesus? The answer is God? Who anoint disciples today, again the answer is God. Every disciple needs the anointing of God. In order to be and do what God has called you, the anointing is essential. The Lord Jesus Christ was who he was and did what he did because of the anointing of God. The anointing

24

empowers you for life and service. You cannot be a disciple and do apostleship without the anointing of God. To be a witness of Jesus Christ and minister of the gospel, you need the anointing of God. To carry the gospel and do the work of the Lord, you need the anointing of God. To be like Christ and do what Christ did, you need the anointing of God. In other words, you must be anointed by God. Two things happened to Jesus: God anointed him with the Holy Spirit and with power, and for God was with him. The anointing of God enabled Jesus to do three things: he went about doing good, he healed people oppressed of the devil and God was with him. When God anoint you, *his goodness, healing and presence* will be yours. Now, you ask, what is the anointing? The anointing is the Holy Spirit and power of God. The anointing is God's nature upon you, and his divine empowerment for service. The reason why you need the anointing: you can be and do in life and service according to the purpose of God. The anointing of God simplifies things for you. The anointing of God makes things easy for you. The anointing is a precious thing. In the Scripture above, I want you to see the anointer, the anointed One and the anointing. God is the anointer. See those words: *how God anointed Jesus.* It is God who anoints disciples. It is God who anoints you and me. The second thing is the Anointed One. The word Christ means the Anointed One or Lord's Anointed. See the words *Jesus of Nazareth.* Jesus is the Christ of God. In Luke 9:17-19, the scripture says:

*And it came to pass, as he was alone praying, his disciples were with him: and he asked them, saying, Whom say the people that I am? They answering said, John the Baptist; but some say, Elias; and others say, that one of the old* prophets *is risen again. He said unto them, But whom say ye that I am? Peter answering said, The Christ of* God.

The Lord Jesus is the Christ of God. The Lord Jesus is the Anointed One. And so are you. You are the anointed disciple. God has given you his Holy Spirit and power. The word Christian does not mean only to belong to Christ or Christ' ones or one like Christ but above all a Christian is anointed disciple. Whatever you do, do not forget Acts 1:8. The Scripture says:

*But ye shall receive power, after that the Holy Ghost is come upon you: and ye shall be witnesses unto me both in Jerusalem, and in all Judaea, and in Samaria, and unto the uttermost part of the earth.*

This is the key verse for the anointing of God. The most important words are receive, the Holy Spirit, power and witness. God wants you to be a disciple by his Holy Spirit and power. To be a disciple and witness the Lord Jesus Christ both in life and service, you need the Holy Spirit and the power of God. Do you want the Holy Spirit and the power of God? I have asked you that question, because some people and places, they do not want the Holy Spirit and the power of God. They receive other things of God but not the Holy Spirit and the power of God. If God gives you the Holy Spirit and his power, what do you do? The answer is very simple you "receive". Many people miss the Holy Spirit and the power of God, because they don't know how to receive from God. To receive from God, you must desire, ask, take interest and be excited for the Holy Spirit and the power.

Take time to thank and praise God for the Holy Spirit and his power and you will receive. Seek God for the Holy Spirit and his power, and you shall receive the anointing of God. The disciples sought God for the Holy Spirit and his power and they received the anointing of God in the Upper Room. The anointing is real. The anointing brings results in your life and service. According to the Holy Bible, there are seven results of the anointing. When God anointed the disciples in the Bible days there were seven things happened to them. The seven results of the anointing are:

1.  Transformation: when Peter received the anointing he was transformed into a new person. Peter who denied the Lord Jesus Christ three times stood up as an eye-witness of Jesus Christ, apostle and minister of the gospel. It is the anointing which makes the difference you need. The anointing transforms you.

2.  Touch: when the Anointing of God comes lives are touched forever. After the anointing came salvation, healing and miracles happened to the people of God. With so many needs to the people of God in modern culture and the $21^{st}$ century, the disciples need to be anointed with the Holy Spirit and power by God.

3.  Boldness: you can be shy, slow to act and fearful, but when the true anointing comes upon you, you will act differently. The disciples were hiding for the fear of the religious leaders and followers, but things changed when they receive the anointing.

The disciples preached the gospel and did the work of the Lord with so much boldness.

4. Grace: Grace is the favour of the Lord. The anointing gives you favour before God and people. Acts 4:33 says these words: *and with great power gave the apostles witness of the resurrection of the Lord Jesus: and great grace was upon them all.* The disciples not only had great power but also great grace. The disciples had great favour in the midst of severe opposition and pressure. As a disciple you need God, great power and great grace to witness Christ.

5. Discipleship: Do you remember the words of Acts 2:41-43? You cannot be a disciple and make so many disciples without the anointing. The anointing makes discipleship possible anywhere in the world. The Scripture says these words*: Then they that gladly received his word were baptized: and the same day there were added unto them about three thousand souls. And they continued stedfastly in the apostles' doctrine and fellowship, and in breaking of bread, and in prayers. And fear came upon every soul: and many wonders and signs were done by the apostles.* To continue stedfastly in the apostles' doctrine (teaching) that is discipleship.

6. Advancement: to go further in the next level with God, you need his anointing. The anointing enables and enhances you. The anointing empowers you to advance forward in the things of the Lord. For example few disciples will become

many. Acts 6:6-7 says these words: *whom they set before the apostles: and when they had prayed, they laid their hands on them. And the word of God increased; and the number of the disciples multiplied in Jerusalem greatly; and a great company of the priests were obedient to the faith.*

7. Establishment: God establish by the anointing. 2 Corinthians 1:21-22. The Scripture says these words: *for all the promises of God in him are yea, and in him Amen, unto the glory of God by us. Now he which stablisheth us with you in* Christ, *and hath anointed us, is God; who hath also sealed us, and given the earnest of the Spirit in our hearts.* In order to be an established disciple you must be anointed by God. You cannot be established without the anointing of God. God establishes you in Christ by his anointing. God establishes you by the Holy Spirit and his power.

## A minister and a disciple

Wherefore I put thee in remembrance that thou stir up the gift of God, which is in thee by the putting on of my hands. For God hath not given us the spirit of fear; but of power, and of love, and of a sound mind.

**2 Timothy 1:6-7**

The minister is servant and mentor. The disciple is follower and a protégé. The good example of this point is the Lord Jesus Christ and the twelve disciples, Paul and Timothy, Barnabas and John Mark, Elijah and Elisha, Moses and

Joshua. When we talk about minister and disciple it is about mentor and protégé. One of the secrets to be a successful in whatever God has called you to be and do, is to have a sound minister and special mentor. Take for example Paul and Timothy. Here we find a minister and a disciple. Paul and Timothy were father and the son in the gospel and work of the Lord. The Scriptures says very clearly in 1Corinthians 4:17, 1 Corinthians 16:10-11 and Philippians 2:22. Firstly, Paul said, Timothy was faithful in the Lord. Secondly, Paul said, Timothy was doing the work of the Lord diligently like him. And thirdly, Paul said, for you know the proof of him, that, as a son with the father, he hath served with me in the gospel. Timothy was successful protégé because he had a special mentor, Paul. Timothy received mentorship and impartation from Paul the apostle. Mentorship and impartation works! In the Scripture above, we see Paul laid his hands upon Timothy and that is impartation. In the work field, Timothy received mentorship in the gospel and work of the Lord. While impartation to Timothy came after Paul laid his hands upon him. Timothy received the impartation of the Spirit. The Holy Spirit is the gift of God. Paul went on to say: God has given us the Spirit of power, love and sound mind. The Holy Spirit is the Spirit of power, love and sound mind. Every disciple needs three things of the Spirit. A disciple need power, love and sound mind. *Notice:* power comes first, then love and sound mind. A disciple is not supposed to be weak but strong. A disciple is not supposed to be fearful but bold for the Spirit. A disciple is not supposed to be idle but diligent for the Spirit in the gospel and the work of the Lord.

Then we see Elijah and Elisha, a minister and a disciple.

Like Timothy, Elisha also received special mentorship and the impartation of the Spirit from Elijah. 2 Kings 2:15 says: now the Spirit of Elijah rest upon Elisha. That was the impartation of the Spirit. Elisha was empowered by the Spirit because he had a minister and a mentor, Elijah. In 1 Kings 19:15-16, God said to Elijah go and anoint Elisha to be a prophet in your place. The word to anoint means to empower by the Spirit. To anoint also means to pass on the mantle. The mantle is symbolic of the Spirit and power of God. In 2 Kings 2:9, Elisha, prayed to Elijah, let the double portion of your Spirit be upon me. And we know his prayer was answered, he received double portion of the Spirit and power, and he served God in the ministry in Israel twice more than Elijah. In Luke 24:49, Jesus said wait in the city, until you are endued with power from on high. In Acts 1:8, Jesus said you shall receive power after the Holy Spirit come upon you. The impartation of the Spirit and power is very important, even Jesus wanted his disciples received it before their greatest work: world apostleship. Who does this impartation? It is God who imparts his Spirit and power in various ways. The impartation of the Spirit and power comes through God himself, his servants and during personal devotion (prayer and the word of God). Finally, we see Moses and Joshua. Joshua also received mentorship and impartation from Moses. In the words of Scripture, Numbers 27:16-18 says:

*"Let the LORD, THE GOD OF THE SPIRITS OF ALL FLESH, SET A MAN OVER THE CONGREGATION, who may go out before them and go in before them, who may lead them out and bring them in, that the congregation of the LORD MAY NOT BE LIKE SHEEP WHICH HAVE NO SHEPHERD." And the LORD SAID TO MOSES: "TAKE JOSHUA THE*

son of Nun WITH YOU, A MAN IN WHOM IS THE SPIRIT, AND LAY YOUR HAND ON HIM.

## Disciples' reference part two

The book of Acts mentioned at least thirty times the term disciple or disciples. The apostles lived and serve God most assuredly as the disciples of Jesus Christ. Disciples' reference will inform you correctly how to be a successful in apostleship and discipleship. Below are disciples' reference points to help you in life from the book of Acts:

1.  Acts 1:1-2,15 World apostleship begins with disciples, the Holy Spirit, commandment of the Lord and things of God set in order

2.  Acts 6:1 disciples needs daily ministration (pastoral care and hospitality)

3.  Acts 6:2 disciples respect world apostleship and the word of God

4.  Acts 6:7 disciples have fresh move of God to multiply

5.  Acts 9:1 disciples are disciples of the Lord Jesus Christ

6.  Acts 9:10-12 a disciple hears the Lord and knows his work

7.  Acts 9:19 a disciple gather together with disciples

8.  Acts 9:25 disciples have got a ministry (helping others)

9. Acts 9:26-27 only a disciple recognise a disciple for world apostleship

10. Acts 9:36 disciples make a good testimony

11. Acts 9:38 disciples welcome world apostleship

12. Acts 11:26 disciples lives with new identity as devoted Christians

13. Acts 11:29 disciples serve God with their giving

14. Acts 13:52 disciples are filled with joy and the Holy Spirit

15. Acts 14:20 disciples are anointed to impact others

16. Acts 141:21 world apostleship includes making great number of disciples

17. Acts 14:22 world apostleship is confirming disciples

18. Acts 14:28 ample time is key to spiritual growth of disciples

19. Acts 15:10 world apostleship brings liberty to new disciples.

20. Acts 16:1-3 world apostleship is mentoring disciples

21. Acts 18:23 world apostleship is strengthening disciples (edifying)

22. Acts 18:27 world apostleship is helping disciples

23. Acts 19:1 finding disciples is part of world apostleship

24. Acts 19:9 world apostleship is to minister the gospel and set apart the disciples

25. Acts 19:30 disciples has a responsibility to defend world apostleship

26. Acts 20:1 disciples needs the anointing (the power of God)

27. Acts 20:7 disciples needs Holy Communion and the word of God

28. Acts 20:30 disciples needs good pastoral work and care

29. Acts 21:4 disciples minister in the Holy Spirit

30. Acts 21:16 disciples do hospitality

## Discipleship and fresh move of the Holy Spirit

And he spake also a parable unto them; No man putteth a piece of a new garment upon an old; if otherwise, then both the new maketh a rent, and the piece that was taken out of the new agreeth not with the old. And no man putteth new wine into old bottles; else the new wine will burst the bottles, and be spilled, and the bottles shall perish. But new wine must be put into new bottles; and both are preserved. No man also having drunk old wine straightway desireth new: for he saith, The old is better.

**Luke 5:36-39**

Let the Holy Spirit move afresh. New wine and new garment is symbolic of fresh move the Holy Spirit. There are some people who said, God moved two thousand years ago, he does not need to move today. What a strange statement to make? There are other people who are focused in the old ways of doing things of God and do not want fresh wave of the Holy Spirit. Looking to the Scripture above, John the Baptist had disciples and Jesus Christ had disciples. Both John and Jesus had divine call, but they served God and ministered differently. There was an accusation to Jesus' ministry that his disciples do not fast and pray. The disciples of Jesus were blamed that they eat and drink all the time. Jesus had to explain the situation in two ways. *Firstly*, he said my disciples don't fast and prayer regularly because the Lord is with them. How do you command my disciples to fast and pray, while the Lord is here? The days are coming when the Lord will ascend back to heaven, then in those days they shall fast and pray. *Secondly*, Jesus explained the situation by the words of Scripture that I have put above. He spoke to them a parable, to differentiate his ministry and apostleship in Israel with that ministry of John the Baptist. Take note: here is where the real task is, God does not change but his move in the gospel and work of the Lord changes. There are two types of the move of God: fresh move and old move. Fresh move is what God is saying and doing now. While old move is how God used to operate. In the old move, what you can do is to learn from it, but you cannot cooperate with God in his old ways while he is saying and doing a new and fresh thing. However, Jesus in his parable has warned, people always like the old move than fresh move. He also said, if you choose old move than fresh move you will struggle and suffer. Not only to move from John's ministry to Jesus ministry and apostleship was difficult. But also to move from law to grace was difficult in Israel. It was difficult also to move from Old Testament to New Testament. Today, it is difficult to move from old culture to modern culture. Or it is difficult to move from old century to 21<sup>st</sup> century. In today modern culture and the 21<sup>st</sup> century there is fresh move of the Holy Spirit. The Holy Spirit is moving afresh in discipleship and apostleship. The Holy Spirit wants us to make new disciples. The Holy Spirit wants to experience fresh touch in the gospel, his work and apostleship. Fresh move of the Holy Spirit is not a strange thing! Fresh move of the Holy Spirit is normal way of doing things by the Lord. In every generation and century the Lord always moved afresh and touched his people in a new way. In his prophecy to the time we are living. Amos prophesied these words:

*Behold, the days come, saith the LORD, that the plowman shall overtake the reaper, and the treader of grapes him that soweth seed; and the mountains shall drop sweet* wine, *and all the hills shall melt.*

Amos's prophecy is about fresh move. The people of God will do things with high speed without limitation. The Holy Spirit fresh move is divine intervention to human limitation. Then the prophecy said the glorious and gracious words: the mountains shall drop sweet wine, and all the hills shall melt. Mountains are bigger than hills. God is bigger than you. Do you remember the words of Abraham when God provided for him a lamb for burnt offering? *He said: And Abraham called the name of that place Jehovah-Jireh: as it is said to this day, In the mount of the LORD it shall be seen.* In other words in the mount of the Lord it shall be provided. In Amos's prophecy, sweet wine speaks of fresh move. God wants you to experience fresh move in far greater level. You may not be able to handle, what God is about to do, for the mountains shall drop sweet wine and the hills shall melt. Be ready for the Lord, something new and fresh is about to take place. In Psalm 92:10, King David said: *but my horn You have exalted like a wild ox; I have been anointed with fresh oil.* Fresh oil is a type of Holy Spirit fresh touch. David was anointed with fresh oil for kingdom and leadership. You are anointed with fresh oil for discipleship and apostleship. You are anointed with fresh oil for the gospel and the work of the Lord. You are anointed with fresh oil to be a disciple. You are anointed with fresh oil to do the things of the Lord. Say, fresh touch! Say, fresh move! Say I believe, I have what the Holy Spirit is saying and doing afresh. Say, loud and clear: I have fresh power and new grace for life and service.

## The anointing for discipleship

And ye are witnesses of these things. And, behold, I send the promise of my Father upon you: but tarry ye in the city of Jerusalem, until ye be endued with power from on high.

**Luke 24:48-49**

The anointing can be received or missed and wasted. The anointing is real. The anointing is a must have power. You need the anointing for discipleship. If the twelve disciples of the Lord Jesus Christ needed the anointing you too need it. You need the Holy Spirit and his power to be a disciple with impact in life and service. The twelve disciples were witnesses of Jesus Christ and ministers of the word, and so you are (Luke 1:2). The twelve disciples needed the Holy Spirit and his power, and so you are (Acts 1:8). The anointing for discipleship is very important. If you understand the term discipleship as to be a disciple and make new disciples, then you cannot do that divine call of God without the Holy Spirit and power from on high. Every person who has a divine call to do something or to be someone needed the Holy Spirit and power from on high. Mary before she could be the mother of the Lord, she needed the Holy Spirit and power from on high. In the words of Scripture, Luke 1:34-35 says:

*Then said Mary unto the angel, How shall this be, seeing I know not a man? And the angel answered and said unto her, The Holy Ghost shall come upon thee, and the power of the Highest shall overshadow thee: therefore also that holy thing which shall be born of thee shall be called the Son of God.*

In verse 37, the angel of God said more to Mary about the call of God for her to be the mother of the Lord. The Scripture records these words: *for with God nothing shall be impossible.* Discipleship is possible! How? Discipleship is possible by the Holy Spirit and the power of the Highest. Discipleship is possible with the Highest (God). And what can I say more, about the Lord Jesus? Dear reader, there is so much to say. The Lord Jesus could not do discipleship and apostleship without the Holy Spirit and power from on high. Luke 3:21-23 says:

*Now when all the people were baptized, it came to pass, that Jesus also being baptized, and praying, the heaven was opened, And the Holy Ghost descended in a bodily shape like a dove upon him, and a voice came from heaven, which said, Thou art my beloved Son; in thee I am well pleased. And Jesus himself began to be about thirty years of age, being (as was supposed) the son of Joseph, which was the son of Heli.*

In the book of Luke there is "power reference" which shows the Lord Jesus was empowered and sent forth by the Holy Spirit. Consider the following "power reference", in verses of Scripture such as: Luke 3:21-23, Luke 4:1,14,18 to19, 32,36 to 37, 38-41, Luke 5:17, Luke 6:19, Luke 8:46, Luke 9:43, Luke 11:20. And the Lord Jesus Christ after his crucifixion and resurrection, he said the most gracious and glorious words in Luke 24:29 and Acts 1:8, the same power I had, it is your time now to receive it. In the words of Scripture, it is written: firstly, tarry ye in the city of Jerusalem until you are *endued with power from on high.* And secondly, you shall *receive power* after *the Holy Spirit come upon you.* How can I receive this power? There are seven ways to receive the power of God which are:

1. The Name of Jesus

2. Impartation

3. Worship

4. The Word of God

5. Wisdom

6. Faith

7. The Holy Spirit

# CHAPTER 3
## *The Holy Spirit and Discipleship*

### Disciples with touch

And the disciples were filled with joy, and with the Holy Ghost

**Acts 13:52**

The need of the Holy Spirit is very clear in the Scriptures. Disciples need to have the Holy Spirit. Disciples in the book of Acts were filled with joy and the Holy Spirit. People respond differently when filled with the Holy Spirit. Some people feel joyful, others weep, and others feel touched by the hand of the Lord. Other people feel heat or fire, others feel the fear of the Lord and others are moved by the presence and power of the Lord. All of these are touching of the Holy Spirit to disciples. The Holy Spirit touches the disciples in different ways. In the Scripture above the disciples were filled with joy and the Holy Spirit. Notice: the disciples were *filled* with *joy* and with *the Holy Spirit*. You need both joy and the Holy Spirit. Not just joy but the Holy Spirit also. Both in Old Testament and New Testament we see joy and the Holy Spirit. The Holy Spirit touched people in both Testaments: Old and New. The Holy Spirit touches people by his presence and power. The book of Acts and the Epistles are the evidence of the presence and power of the Holy Spirit. The results of the presence of the Holy Spirit are: **firstly**, the touch of God. The presence brings the touch of God. **Secondly**, the presence releases the voice of God. The presence makes people sensitive to the voice of God. **Thirdly**, the presence releases the power of God. The presence is the key to the power of God. Time spent in the presence of God is not time wasted. **Fourthly**, the presence brings the character of God. The Bible says this character of God is the fruit of the Spirit (Galatians 5:22-23). **Fifthly,** the presence brings the call of God. The Holy Spirit calls people while they are in the presence of God. The good example of this point is Acts 13:2. The presence of the Holy Spirit is so important. When the Holy Spirit enters your life, these five things will happen in your life.

In 1 Thessalonians 1:5-6, we see the disciples in Thessalonica regardless of afflictions of salvation, yet they were received the word with joy of the Holy Spirit. The Apostle Paul said when they went to Thessalonica, their gospel was not in word only but also in power, in the Holy Spirit and in much assurance. Then the people became followers (disciples) of the apostles and the Lord. When the people became followers they were persecuted because they received word. The Holy Spirit did not allowed the disciples to be sad and left salvation, but they had the joy of the Holy Spirit. The joy of the Holy Spirit helps you to stand against afflictions of the word. In the words of Scripture, the Scripture says:

*For our gospel came not unto you in word only, but also in power, and in the Holy Ghost, and in much assurance; as ye know what manner of men we were among you for your sake. And ye became followers of us, and of the Lord, having received the word in much affliction, with joy of the Holy Ghost.*

The Holy Spirit is the Spirit of Joy. The Holy Spirit brings joy. Even in Old Testament we see joy is linked with the Holy Spirit. Psalms 51:10-12 shows the Holy Spirit, presence and joy of salvation. Psalm 16:11 says in your presence there is fullness of joy. In you right hand there pleasures for evermore. When you know the Holy Spirit and his presence then joy is yours. Joy is one of the touches of the Holy Spirit. Disciples are people touched by the Holy Spirit and his joy. Disciples are both saved and filled with the Holy Spirit. Both salvation and the Holy Spirit are important to disciples. There is the joy of salvation and joy of the Holy Spirit.

## Filled and led by the Holy Spirit

And be not drunk with wine, wherein is excess; but be filled with the Spirit;

**Ephesians 5:18**

The Spirit! Yes, filled with the Spirit. The Spirit is the Holy Spirit. God desire for you is to be filled and led by the Holy Spirit. A disciple must be filled and led by the Holy Spirit. Even in Old Testament, King David knew the leading of the Spirit. Psalm 143:10 says your Spirit is good; lead me into the land of uprightness. The Holy Spirit led King David. King David knew the Holy Spirit, his presence and voice.

David was sensitive to the things of the Spirit. Another place we see the infilling of the Spirit is Exodus 31:2-3. God spoke to Moses, He said, see I have called Bezaleel and look I have filled him with the Spirit of God. The Spirit of God is the Holy Spirit. People in the Bible days were filled and led by the Spirit. Galatians 5:18 says about being led by the Spirit. In the words of Scripture, The Scripture says:

*But if ye be led of the Spirit, ye are not under the law.*

A disciple of Jesus Christ needs to be filled and led by the Holy Spirit. A disciple cannot afford to live without the Spirit. What is Pentecostal experience? Or what is Upper Room experience? Pentecostal experience or Upper Room experience is about being filled and led by the Spirit. Pentecostal experience or Upper Room experience is not about a church sign or name but the Holy Spirit in you. When you are filled and led by the Holy Spirit that itself is total experience. You do not need top up. What is being filled and led by the Spirit? That Holy Spirit experience means the Holy Spirit is in total control and in charge of your life. To be filled with the Spirit means the Holy Spirit has entered your life. The Holy Spirit now lives in you. To be led by the Spirit means the Spirit guides you. This is the highest level of the Holy Spirit. The first level is to be filled by the Spirit. The second level is to be led by the Spirit. In the book of Acts, disciples were filled and led by the Spirit. *The first example* is Peter. Peter was filled by the Spirit in Acts 2:4, and then led by the Spirit in Acts 10:19-20. Peter was both filled and led by the Spirit. *The second example* is Paul. Paul was filled by the Spirit in Acts 9:17 and was led by the Spirit in Acts 16:6-10. Paul also was filled and led by the Spirit. *The third example* is the disciples at Galatia. Paul wrote to them you began in the Spirit, do not be fulfilled in the flesh. That statement means they were saved and filled with the Spirit (Galatians 3:2-3). In Galatians 5:18, Paul wrote to them: if you are led by the Spirit you are not under the law. The disciples in Galatia were both filled and led by the Spirit. The problem was they left grace and went back into law, and forgot what God has done in their live by the gospel (Galatians 1:6). God was so good to the disciples at the Galatians church. God did miracles and supplied them with the Holy Spirit (Galatians 3:5). The Holy Spirit wants to fill and lead your life. An empty life is not the will of the Lord. The Lord wants you to be filled and led by the Spirit. Are you ready to be filled and led by the Spirit? Say, yes to the Holy Spirit. Mathew 5:6 is the key verse if you want this gracious and glorious Holy Spirit experience. The Scripture says: blessed are they who hunger and thirty for righteousness; for they shall be filled. If you desire salvation and the Holy Spirit, the Lord shall fill you.

## The Holy Spirit then and now

Disciples need to understand there is one Holy Spirit. The Holy Spirit has not changed. The Holy Spirit in the gospels, book of Acts, the epistles and book of Revelation is still the same. There is no two or three Holy Spirit but one Holy Spirit. The Holy Spirit who came upon the Lord Jesus Christ, the disciples and apostles is the same. The Holy Spirit we have is the same Holy Spirit they had. The problem may be the Lord, disciples and apostles knew better about the person and work of the Holy Spirit than us. If you do not know the person and work of the Holy Spirit, you will struggle. The work of the Holy Spirit is found in the book of Acts but also in the Epistles of Apostles. The work of the Holy Spirit is both to the world and the church. The Holy Spirit has work in the world and in the church. The condition of the world and the church concerns the Lord. The Holy Spirit has two works: apostleship and discipleship. These two works of the Holy Spirit were for then and now. Is apostleship for today? Yes. Is discipleship for today? Yes. The most important thing is to understand, what is apostleship? And what is discipleship? Apostleship in simple terms is sending away for the gospel and work of the Lord. Discipleship is making disciples of the Lord and following Jesus Christ. When you understand the person and work of the Holy Spirit, then all things of the Lord become easy. Along with apostleship and discipleship, the Holy Spirit work is also to the lost and found people of God. To the sinner the Holy Spirit witness Christ and testify the gospel of God. While on the other hand, to the saint the Holy Spirit transforms disciples and glorifies the Lord Jesus Christ. The Holy Spirit also establishes the disciples as first-fruit of the Spirit, bring forth the fruit of the Spirit, manifest the gifts of the Spirits and give forth the ministry gifts of the Lord. These are works of the Spirit done to the disciples (saved ones). Now let us find out what it means to each one of these works of the Spirit.

## First fruits of the Spirit

And not only they, but ourselves also, which have the firstfruits of the Spirit, even we ourselves groan within

Benjamin Maira

ourselves, waiting for the adoption, to wit, the redemption of
our body. For we are saved by hope: but hope that is seen is
not hope: for what a man seeth, why doth he yet hope for?

**Romans 8:23-24**

The work of the Holy Spirit is your initial salvation. The
Spirit works in the life of a disciple. The Holy Spirit work is
not about ministry and no salvation at all. The work of the
Spirit is both salvation and ministry. What is first-fruits of
the Spirit? First of all, first-fruits of the Spirit is about the
first harvest. In the Old Testament times, when farmers
gathered the first harvest, the first harvest belonged unto the
Lord. Even the first child was called Holy unto the Lord.
Parents will take the child to the temple and present him
unto the Lord. Even when the Lord Jesus Christ was born,
he was taken to the temple and presented to the Lord (Luke
2:22-23). Now this was very practical, but today is all things
of the Lord are done in the Spirit. When a person is saved, he
is first-fruit of the Spirit. When a person is saved, he is first
born unto the Lord. The Lord Jesus Christ has this status. In
Romans 8:29, he is called the firstborn among the brethren.
In 1 Corinthians 15:23, Christ is called first-fruits. Therefore
first-fruits to every disciple, means he has been given the
same identity of Christ. As Christ is firstborn and first-fruit
so you are. Jesus Christ is our Lord and brother. And we
are many brothers and sisters in the Lord. First-fruits of
the Spirit mean the Holy Spirit is the foretaste of the life to
come. Your salvation is God's pledge that you receive full
adoption as a child and heir of God. Every child of God is
part of the full harvest of the Lord to come. In the words of
Scripture: James 1:18 says: *Of his own will begat he us with*

*the* word of truth, *that we should be a kind of firstfruits of his creatures.*

## The Fruit of the Spirit

But the fruit of the Spirit is love, joy, peace, longsuffering, gentleness, goodness, faith, Meekness, temperance: against such there is no law.

### Galatians 5:22-23

The fruit of the Spirit is different with first-fruits of the Spirit. While the first-fruits of the Spirit is about your initial salvation, the fruit of the Spirit is the result of salvation. The fruit of the Spirit is character. The Holy Spirit produces forth character. The fruit of the Spirit is the result of the Holy Spirit and his presence in your life. How do you know you have the Holy Spirit and his presence? There are five evidences to know you have the Holy Spirit: *firstly*, you know you have the Holy Spirit by faith (Galatians 3:2-3,5). *Secondly*, you know you have the Holy Spirit by the gift of speaking in tongues (Acts 19:6-7). The Holy Spirit is not tongues but a person. Tongues are outward manifestation of the inward person, who is the Holy Spirit. *Thirdly*, you know you have the Holy Spirit by the evidence of personal life transformation. For example Paul was transformed from Saul the murderer to Paul the apostle (Acts 13:9). *Fourthly,* you know you have the Holy Spirit by the fruit of the Spirit. When the nine flavours of the fruit of the Spirit are evident in your life, like love, joy and peace, you know the Holy Spirit is inside you (Romans 5:5 and Romans 14:17). *Fifthly*:

you know you have the Holy Spirit, because the word of God says so. 2 Timothy 1:14 says:

*That good thing which was committed unto thee keep by the Holy Ghost which dwelleth in us.*

So you see the fruit of the Spirit is very important. The fruit of the Spirit is the evidence you have the Holy Spirit. A disciple with the character of the Spirit is the disciple who has the Holy Spirit. People who will inherit the kingdom of God are people who have the fruit of the Spirit not the works of the flesh. The Fruit of the Spirit is divided in into three groups: *God, other and you.* Related to God is about love, joy and peace. Related to others is about patience, gentleness and goodness. Related to you is about faithfulness, meekness and self-control. The fruit of the Sprit is also about the Holy Trinity. In Ephesians 5:9 we read: *for the* fruit *of the Spirit is in all goodness and righteousness and truth.* Goodness: we know is about God. God is good. God is good to all people. Righteousness: we know is about righteousness in the Lord Jesus Christ. Righteousness is obtained by faith in the Lord Jesus Christ. Truth: we know is about the Holy Spirit. The Holy Spirit is the Spirit of truth. Disciples need to have the fruit of the Spirit for the Lord. Ephesians 5:10 says: *proving what is acceptable unto the Lord.* What is acceptable unto the Lord is not the works of the flesh but the fruit of the Spirit. What is acceptable unto the Lord is character.

## The gifts of the Spirit

For to one is given by the Spirit the word of wisdom; to another the word of knowledge by the same Spirit; To another faith by the same Spirit; to another the gifts of healing by the same Spirit; To another the working of miracles; to another prophecy; to another discerning of spirits; to another divers kinds of tongues; to another the interpretation of tongues:

## 1 Corinthians 12:8-10

The gifts of the Spirit are commonly known as spiritual gifts (1 Corinthians 12:1). What are the spiritual gifts? The gifts of the Spirit are defined as *special abilities* by the Spirit. Along with prayer and the ministry of the word, there are the gifts of the Spirit. You can serve God and minister in the gifts of the Spirit. The gifts of the Spirits are nine gifts. The gifts of the Spirit are listed in 1 Corinthians 12:8-10. Although there are nine gifts but there is one Holy Spirit. There is one Holy Spirit and nine gifts (1 Corinthians 12:4). There are different gifts but the same the Spirit. There are diversities of administrations but the same the Lord. And there are different operations but the same God. Notice, the Holy Trinity of God: the Spirit, the Lord and God. Ministers of the gospel do not minister the same way but the same God who works in all. What is the purpose of the gifts of the Spirit? The purpose of the gifts of the Spirit is to the profit of all disciples and people. Verse seven says: *but the manifestation of the Spirit is given to each one to the profit of all.* The gifts of the Spirit are not for boasting or selfishness. The gifts of the Spirit are for two reasons. First reason: world apostleship and discipleship (Mark 16:15,20 and Mark 6:7,12-13). Second reason: for edifying of the church of the Lord (1 Corinthians 14:12). What is the key to serve God and minister in the gifts of the Spirit? The key is the *Holy Spirit, power and the voice of God.* Another key is praise and worship to God. Praise and worship brings the presence of God in action. When the atmosphere is super charged by the presence and power of God then the Spirit will manifest his gifts. Praise and worship is the master key to the atmosphere of the Spirit and his presence before the gifts are displayed in a public scene.

There gifts of the Spirit can be divided into three groups: *the gifts of revelation, the gifts of deeds (power) and the gifts of speech.* Group one: the gifts of revelation are *word of wisdom, word of knowledge and discerning of the spirits.* The gifts of revelation are called so because they reveal something to disciples. Group two: the gifts of power. The gifts of power are *faith, gifts of healing and the working of miracles.* The gifts of power demonstrate the power of God. The gifts of speech are *prophecy, divers kinds of tongue and interpretation of tongues.* The gifts of speech communicate something from the Lord. All nine gifts are the work of the same Spirit (1 Corinthians 12:11).

## Ministry gifts of the Lord

And he gave some, apostles; and some, prophets; and some, evangelists; and some, pastors and teachers; For the perfecting of the saints, for the work of the ministry, for the edifying of the body of Christ:

**Ephesians 4:11-12**

The ministry gifts of the Lord are set forth by the Holy Spirit as apostles, prophets, evangelists, pastors and teachers. Notice: there are five ministry gifts not four. The pastor is not a mixed gift of pastor-teacher. The pastor is not one ministry gift with that of a teacher. Notice: there were teachers in Antioch (Acts 13:1). There were teachers in Corinth (1 Corinthians 12:28) and there were teachers in Ephesus. A pastor is able to teach but not a teacher by divine call (2 Timothy 2:23-24). A pastor is called, empowered and set forth by the Holy Spirit to shepherd the sheep. A pastor is a sound minister in the Local church (1Timothy 4:6). Then we have the ministry gift of an evangelist. The term evangelist appears in the Bible three times (Acts 21:8, Ephesians 4:11 and 2 Timothy 4:5). There is a mixture of ideas and human opinions, some people say, the task of an evangelist is relatively unknown. What a strange statement a person to make! Off-course the task of an evangelist is known. *Who is an evangelist?* The evangelist is a preacher of the gospel. The evangelist preaches Christ and what he has done on the cross. The evangelist wins souls to the Lord. The evangelist is a travelling missionary. The evangelist preaches the gospel with healing and miracles. *Who is a prophet?* A prophet is a voice, messenger, and spokesman of God. A prophet is a servant of the Lord, an inspired preacher and seer. A prophet is a man of God might in speech and deed. The term prophet means *one set forth* by God. Prophets not only prophesy but they can preach, teach and work. A prophet is a minister of the gospel. Just like in any ministry gift there are two types of the prophets: *false and true prophets. Who is an apostle?* An apostle is a special messenger, a chosen vessel and an ambassador the gospel with signs and wonders. An apostle is a commissioner of Christ. An apostle is a minister and witness of the Lord Jesus Christ. An apostle is divinely called, empowered and sent forth by the Holy Spirit. An Apostle is *one sent forth* by God. Just like in any other ministry gift there are false and true apostles.

The ministry gifts of the Lord are divine call (Ephesians 4:1). In other words you serve God and minister to people by divine call. You must be called by the Lord. Who call these ministry gifts into the service of God? Not man or a committee but the Lord. In the words of Scripture, Ephesians 4:8 says: He gave gifts unto men. Who? It is the Lord. Also we see in Acts 13:1-5,47, that the Holy Spirit call the servants of God to minister the gospel and do the work of the Lord (apostleship). It is the Holy Spirit who calls, empowers and sends, men and women to the work of the Lord. What are the keys to serve God in the ministry gifts? There are five keys to serve God in the ministry gifts. One of the keys is the Holy Spirit. *First key*: the Holy Spirit. *The second key*: sound minister. You must have a sound minister if you are to serve the Lord in the ministry gifts. *Third key*: the local church. If you are to serve the Lord in the ministry gifts you need the local church. *Fourth key*: prayer and *fifth key* is the word of God. The ministry gifts serve God by prayer and the word of God. The ministry gifts perfect the saints (disciples) to do the work of the ministry. The ministry gifts deals with things lacking in the life of disciples. The ministry gifts nurture and mature the disciples of the Lord. Without the ministry gifts a disciple cannot do well in the gospel and work of the Lord. Today more than ever we need the five ministry gifts of the Lord.

## The Holy Spirit and disciples in the book of Acts

Since the coming of the Spirit in the book of Acts, the Holy Spirit has made his work known and advances it. The Holy Spirit came upon one disciple after another. The disciples received the Spirit and they knew him and his work. Can the Holy Spirit do the same as to disciples of the book of Acts? Oh! Yes. The Spirit still speaks and works today. The disciples of today must give open space to the Spirit, for him to speak and work among them. The Spirit is unlimited to age, culture and generation. The Spirit speaks and works all the time, any place and to any group of people. What is precondition for people is to be open to the Holy Spirit, his power and voice. If people do so, they will experience the Holy Spirit in disciple's life. Now we are going to find out in every chapter of the book of Acts, an insight of the Holy Spirit: who he is and how he speak and work from the book of Acts to our present generation.

1.  Chapter one: the Holy Spirit was with disciples before Pentecost, Acts 1:2,15-16

2.  Chapter two: the Holy Spirit filled the disciples, Acts 2:4

3.  Chapter three: the Holy Spirit brought times of refreshing, Acts 3:19

4.  Chapter four: the Holy Spirit filled the disciples with boldness, power and grace, Acts 4:29-31,33

5.  Chapter five: the Holy Spirit made known his deity and duty. He is God and show forth secrets of men and women. Acts 5:3-4,9

6. Chapter six: the Holy Spirit works miracles, speaks and changes disciples, Acts 6:8,10,15

7. Chapter seven: the Holy Spirit show forth the glory of God, Acts 7:1-2,55-56

8. Chapter eight: the Holy Spirit is powerful, Acts 8:6,29

9. Chapter nine: the Holy Spirit fills Paul and bring comfort to the disciples, Acts 9:17,31

10. Chapter ten: the Holy Spirit led Peter, and made Cornelius a disciple and all his house , Acts 10:19-20

11. Chapter eleven: the Holy Spirit visited Cornelius and his house, Acts 11:15

12. Chapter twelve: the Holy Spirit rescue Peter from Prison, Acts 12:17

13. Chapter thirteen: the Holy Spirit changed Paul, Acts 13:9

14. Chapter fourteen: the Holy Spirit granted signs and wonders to be done, Acts 14:3

15. Chapter fifteen: the Holy Spirit is pleased with the disciples, Acts 15:28-29

16. Chapter sixteen: the Holy Spirit led Paul, Silas and Timothy to preach the gospel and do the work of the Lord, Acts 16:6-10

17. Chapter seventeen: The Holy Spirit made impact with disciples, Acts 17:3-4

18. Chapter eighteen: the Holy Spirit draw many disciples, Acts 18:7-11

19. Chapter nineteen: the Holy Spirit touch disciples in a unique way, Acts 19:1-7

20. Chapter twenty: the Holy Spirit witnesses to Paul and made leaders, Acts 20:23,28

21. Chapter twenty one: the Holy Spirit uses disciples, Acts 21:4-5

22. Chapter twenty two: the Holy Spirit send Paul to the far parts of the world for apostleship and discipleship, Acts 22:21

23. Chapter three: The Holy Spirit is practical and rescue Paul in a special way, Acts 23:16-18,

24. Chapter twenty four: The Holy Spirit use disciples to declare faith in Christ, Acts 24:24-25

25. Chapter twenty five: The Holy Spirit use disciples to affirm the living Christ, Acts 25:19

26. Chapter twenty six: the Holy Spirit at the pick of world apostleship and discipleship, Acts 26:22-23

27. Chapter twenty seven: The Holy Spirit declares all is well and safe journey, Acts 27:23-25

28. Chapter twenty eight: the Holy Spirit is the source of salvation and healing, Acts 28:7-10, 28

## The dispensation of the Holy Spirit

That he would grant you, according to the riches of his glory, to be strengthened with might by his Spirit in the inner man

**Ephesians 3:16**

When God gave grace he also gave the Holy Spirit. With grace of the Lord Jesus Christ, came also the Holy Spirit. What a privilege do we have? God gave not only His Son to the disciples but also His Spirit. Do you realize how privileged you are! You have the Holy Spirit in fullness. The Lord of the universe, our Father and God has given you all he ever had: the Son and the Spirit. The term dispensation is a strong term. Dispensation does not only mean a period of time of grace but also the giving of the Holy Spirit, privilege, special consideration (the Lord's favour), relaxation of the rules (from law to grace) and exemption. The giving of the Holy Spirit in the New Testament is a great experience of the Lord. For years prophet after prophet prophesied the coming of the Spirit. And here we are, you and me, we see and hear the Holy Spirit has arrived, he is real and bring great results in disciples life. What we have is the Spirit without measure. This is, if you will agree, the age of the Spirit and giving of the Spirit. The just and holy men of ancient world did not have the Spirit as you and I have him today. In the past, God only gave the Holy Spirit to his servants not to all people. But he gave prophecies to his prophets: Moses, Isaiah, Joel. God said: the days are coming; I will pour out my Spirit upon all people. And upon my servants (men and women) I pour out of my Spirit. In the words of Scripture, Acts 2:16-18 says:

*And it shall come to pass afterward, that I will pour out my spirit upon all flesh; and your sons and your daughters shall prophesy, your old men shall dream dreams, your young men shall see visions: and also upon the servants and upon the handmaids in those days will I pour out my spirit.*

That time is now. Now is the time of the Spirit. God does look upon age and gender any more. All people can receive the Spirit. God gives the Spirit not according to men's opinion or idea but according to the riches of his glory. The apostle Paul prayed for the disciples at Ephesus (see above Scripture), that God will grant to them, according to the riches of his glory that they be strengthen with might, in the inner man. The Holy Spirit strengthen disciples in the inner most being. Our focus should not be men, doctrine of men and men practice but the Holy Spirit sovereignty. The Holy Spirit is able to do things man cannot do. For with God nothing shall be impossible, the Scripture says. **Who is the Spirit?** The Holy Spirit is a unique being. The Holy Spirit according to the Scriptures he is **sweet, smart, strong, sovereign, source, Spirit and sent by God.** In Galatians 4:6, Paul said: *and because ye are sons, God hath sent forth the Spirit of his Son into your hearts, crying, Abba, Father.*

The person and work of the Holy Spirit is very clear in these seven points. *Point one*: the Holy Spirit is sweet Spirit. That means the Spirit is good and gracious. The Scripture says test and see the Lord is good and gracious. *Point two*: the Holy Spirit is smart. That means the Holy Spirit is intelligent and sensitive. The Scripture says the Spirit teaches, reveals and knows the things of God. *Point three*: the Holy Spirit is Strong. That means the Spirit is not weak but he is the Spirit of strength and might. The Scripture says, you shall receive power after the Holy Spirit comes upon you. *Point four*: the Holy Spirit is sovereign. That means the Spirit is divine with authority which is evident in the Scriptures. *Point five*: the Holy Spirit is source. Nothing happens without the Holy Spirit. The Scripture says, not by might nor by power but by my Spirit. *Point six*: the Holy Spirit is Spirit being. The Holy Spirit is not angelic or human but the Spirit. The Holy Spirit is the Spirit being. *Point seven*: the Holy Spirit is sent by God. The Spirit did not come by himself, he is sent by God. The Scripture above says: God has sent forth the Spirit of his Son unto your hearts, crying, Abba, Father.

## The Holy Spirit and disciples in the Epistles

Ye are our epistle written in our hearts, known and read of all men: Forasmuch as ye are manifestly declared to be the epistle of Christ ministered by us, written not with ink, but with the Spirit of the living God; not in tables of stone, but in fleshy tables of the heart.

**2 Corinthians 3:2-3**

From the epistles of 1 Corinthians, 2 Corinthians, Galatians and Ephesians we find the Holy Spirit working in disciples' life. In other words the Spirit works in your life and mine. In 2 Corinthians 3:16-18, there is glorious work of the Spirit for the disciples from these precious verses of Scripture. Three things are mention: one, the Spirit takes away the veil of blindness in the heart of a disciple. Two, the Spirit dwells with disciples and brings liberty to disciples. Three, the Spirit transforms disciples life according to the glory of the Lord. Then, we also find great work of the Spirit in disciples' salvation from Galatians 3:1-3 and 1 Corinthians 12:2-3. As you read on the list of the work of the Spirit, you will discover other works of the Spirit in disciple's life.

1. The Holy Spirit deal with disciples heart, 2 Corinthians 3:2-3

2. The Holy Spirit make disciples living epistles of Christ, 2 Corinthians 3:2-3

3. The Holy Spirit speak and minister to disciples, 2 Corinthians 3:2-3

4. The Holy Spirit make disciples able ministers of the Spirit, 2 Corinthians 3:6

5. The Holy Spirit bring glorious ministry of the Spirit to disciples, 2 Corinthians 3:8-9

6. The Holy Spirit takes away the veil in disciples heart, 2 Corinthians 3:16

7. The Holy Spirit bring liberty to disciples, 2 Corinthians 3:17

8. The Holy Spirit transforms disciples from glory to glory, 2 Corinthians 3:18

9. The Holy Spirit is connected to disciples, 1 Corinthians 6:17

10. The Holy Spirit commune with disciples, 2 Corinthians 13:14

11. The Holy Spirit fill disciples, Ephesians 5:18

12. The Holy Spirit lead disciples, Galatians 5:18

13. The Holy Spirit is the guarantee of the Spirit to disciples, 2 Corinthians 5:5

14. The Holy Spirit give disciples access to the Father, Ephesians 2:18

15. The Holy Spirit build disciples as habitation of God, Ephesians 2:22

16. The Holy Spirit reveal Christ to disciples, Ephesians 3:5-7

17. The Holy Spirit strengthen disciples, Ephesians 3:16

18. The Holy Spirit unify disciples, Ephesians 4:3-4

19. The Holy Spirit give grace to disciples, Ephesians 4:7

20. The Holy Spirit uses the word of God in disciples life, Ephesians 6:17

21. The Holy Spirit uses prayer in disciples life, Ephesians 6:18

22. The Holy Spirit does great work of disciples' salvation, Galatians 3:1-3

23. The Holy Spirit comes to disciples, Galatians 3:5

24. The Holy Spirit gives to disciples presence and fruit of the Spirit, Galatians 5:22-23

25. The Holy Spirit gives to disciples power and gifts of the Spirit, 2 Corinthians 12:7-10

26. The Holy Spirit gives to disciples divine call and ministry gifts of the Lord, Ephesians 4:7,11-12

# CHAPTER 4
## Discipleship and good report

Disciples are well reported

Then came he to Derbe and Lystra: and, behold, a certain disciple was there, named Timotheus, the son of a certain woman, which was a Jewess, and believed; but his father was a Greek: Which was well reported of by the brethren that were at Lystra and Iconium. Him would Paul have to go forth with him; and took and circumcised him because of the Jews which were in those quarters: for they knew all that his father was a Greek

**Acts 16:1-3**

Paul found Timothy and took him to go forth with him. Certain things are mentioned of Timothy. He was a disciple, who believed and well reported by the brethren. Paul must have been pleased to hear good report of Timothy. A good report is a good thing to a disciple. A good report brings divine connection with sound ministers of the gospel. A disciple must be a believer with good report before the Lord and the brethren. A disciple as we have seen in New Testament is not just a student but a believer with good report. If Timothy was not a believer and with good report; Paul could not took him and go forth with him in the gospel and work of the Lord. How you conduct yourself before the Lord and the brethren is very important. Discipleship is the Lord's call. Good report is about good character. Timothy had both. Too many people have the Lord's call but lack good character. You find disciples with the Lord's call but with bad character. You need to have both the Lord's call and good character. Character is everything. Everywhere you go character is highly required (good report). In the first early church in Jerusalem the apostles wanted seven men to do hospitality and helping of the poor saints. Peter the apostle gave a list of three things required: *a good report, the Holy Spirit and wisdom.* You see good report is required everywhere you go. In the words of Scripture, Acts 6:3 says: *wherefore, brethren, look ye out among you seven men of honest report, full of the Holy Ghost and* wisdom*, whom we may appoint over this business.* Every disciple need to have good report, the Holy Spirit and wisdom. Did Timothy have all three things: good report, the Holy Spirit and wisdom? The answer is yes. Acts 16:2 says Timothy was well reported of by the brethren. 2 Timothy 1:14 says Timothy had the Holy Spirit. And 2 Timothy 3:15 says that the Scriptures which Timothy have known since he was a child are able to make him wise. In personal discipleship, you need to have good report, the Holy Spirit and wisdom. Take Paul the apostle for example, he too, in his work and apostleship he had good report, the Holy Spirit and wisdom. 1 Corinthians 4:17 says Paul had goof report. In 1 Corinthians 7:40, Paul said I think, I also I have the Spirit of God. In 1 Corinthians 3:10,

Paul said he is a wise master builder and have laid down one foundation, and that foundation is the Lord Jesus Christ.

## The seven keys to personal discipleship

In the Holy Scriptures there are seven important things to personal discipleship. I call them the seven keys to personal discipleship. In these keys to personal discipleship we are going to focus our attention to Timothy who was a disciple and workfellow with Paul. Paul called Timothy my workfellow in Romans 16:21. Paul called Timothy our brother, minister of God and fellow labourer in the gospel of Christ in 1 Thessalonians 3:1-2. Paul called Timothy a witness in 2 Timothy 2:2. Paul called Timothy a sound minister in the church of the Lord in 1 Timothy 1:3-4 and 1 Timothy 4:6. If you read Romans 16, you will find out Paul's team in the gospel and work of the Lord. In this great chapter Paul wrote a big list of names of men and women. In this big and best list of men and women of God he showed their work and his relationship to them. But among all these men and women of God, Timothy was unique and of different class to him. Timothy serve as son with father in the gospel (Philippians 2:22) Timothy was diligent in the work of the Lord (1 Corinthians 16:10). And Timothy was faithful in the Lord (1 Corinthians 4:17). Timothy was a disciple, minister and brother to the great apostle of the Lord, Paul. In the gospel and work of the Lord it is believed Timothy was an evangelist, pastor and teacher. The Scriptures shows he was a proven evangelist who worked diligently in 2 Timothy 4:5, he was a sound pastor in the local church at Ephesus (1 Timothy 1:3-4) and a strong teacher (2 Timothy 4:2-3). You must know Timothy was a protégé and Paul was a mentor. Timothy was a successor and Paul was a predecessor. The mantle for the gospel and work of the Lord was passed on from Paul to Timothy. Everything you know about Paul including his sound knowledge and ministry skills was imparted to Timothy. This is why Paul took time to write two epistles (1Timothy and 2 Timothy) about pastoral ministry and local church. It is through this young man Timothy we find the seven keys to personal discipleship.

What are seven keys to personal discipleship? The seven keys to person discipleship are:

1. **The Holy Spirit**: Timothy knew the Holy Spirit. Timothy had the Holy Spirit inside of him. And Paul knew about the Holy Spirit dwelt in Timothy. It was the Holy Spirit who made Timothy a key disciple and a brother in the Lord. If you are going to be a key disciple and strong Christian, you can't be and do that without the Holy Spirit. The Holy Spirit is the Spirit of power, love and sound mind. See 2 Timothy 1:7,14

2. **Faith**: Timothy was a believer. Timothy had faith in the Lord. Faith is very important to stand with the Lord. Faith is a gift of the Spirit, faith is a key to salvation, faith is a weapon in spiritual warfare and faith is a ministry tool to hear the gospel and see healing and miracles. Faith is real. A disciple of the Lord need to have faith and you will not faint, fail and fall down. See, 2 Timothy 1:5

3. **Witness**: Timothy was a witness and sound minister of the gospel. In 2 Timothy 2:2, Paul told Timothy these words: *And the things that thou hast heard of me among many witnesses, the same commit thou to faithful men, who shall be able to teach others also.* The gospel and work of the Lord is taking what is already available and pass on to faithful men and women. It is not about looking for new things or your own things all the time. Timothy was also a sound minister of the gospel. See, 1 Timothy 4:6.

4. **Prayer:** Timothy was a man of prayer. Every disciple needs to be a man or woman of prayer. In the words of Scripture, 1 Timothy 2:8-10 says: *I will therefore that men pray everywhere, lifting up* holy hands, *without wrath and doubting. In like manner also, that women adorn themselves in modest apparel, with shamefacedness and sobriety; not with broided hair, or gold, or* pearls, *or costly array; But (which becometh women professing godliness) with good works.* Men are instructed to pray and lifting holy hands without sin (wrath and doubting). Women too are commanded to pray, look after themselves and do good works.

5. **The word of God:** Timothy knew the word of God since he was a child. In the words of scripture, 2 Timothy 3:15-17 says: *and that from a child thou hast known the* Holy Scriptures, *which are able to make thee wise unto salvation through faith which is in* Christ Jesus. All scripture is given by inspiration *of God, and is profitable for*

*doctrine, for reproof, for correction, for instruction in righteousness: that the man of God may be perfect, thoroughly furnished unto all good works.* The Holy Scriptures are the very words of God. A man of God is made perfect and thoroughly furnished unto good works by the very words of God. The word of God enables you to be a good disciple.

6. **Good report**: Timothy was well reported of by the brethren, see Acts 16:1-3. A good report is a good thing to a disciple. A good report brings divine connection with sound ministers of the gospel. A disciple must be a believer with good report before the Lord and the brethren. A disciple as we have seen in New Testament is not just a student but a believer with good report. If Timothy was not a believer and with good report; Paul could not take him and go forth with him in the gospel and work of the Lord. How you conduct yourself before the Lord and the brethren is very important.

7. **Impartation**: Timothy received impartation from Paul, the church elders, his mother Eunice and Grandmother Lois. Timothy was brought up in a family of faith in the Lord. His grandmother and mother imparted faith upon him. Then though Paul and the group of elders the three precious gifts of God: salvation, the Holy Spirit and ministry was imparted to him. See, 1 Timothy 4:14 and 2 Timothy 1:5-7

## Report reference

Let us see the report reference in the epistles. I have chosen few Scriptures to show key insights for the word report in the New Testament. Every disciple can have a good report and magnify the Lord. The report reference is found in:

1. Acts 4:23-24. Report to the company of disciples and pray to God.
2. Acts 6:3. A disciple needs good report, the Holy Spirit and wisdom.
3. Acts 10:22. A disciple must be devoted, one who fear God and of good report.
4. Acts 16:2. A disciple is a person well reported by the brethren.
5. Acts 22:12. A disciple must be devoted to the word of God and with good report.
6. Romans 10:16. A disciple believes on the report of the gospel.
7. 1 Corinthians 14:25. A good report to none disciples.
8. 2 Corinthians 6:8. A disciple stand in the Lord regardless of what he faces.
9. Philippians 4:8. Every disciple must have all things and good report.
10. 1 Timothy 3:7. A disciple must have a good report of them which are without.
11. 1 Timothy 5:10. A disciple must be well reported of, for good works.

12. Hebrews 11:2. A disciple can obtain good report by faith.

13. Hebrews 11:39. A disciple can obtain both good report and the promises of God.

14. 1 Peter 1:12. The gospel reports the things of the Lord to a disciple.

15. 3 John 1:12. A disciple has good report among all men in all truth and bear a true record

Prayer, the Holy Spirit and the word of God for a disciple

In his discipleship and apostleship to Israel the Lord Jesus Christ did it through prayer, the Holy Spirit and the word of God. Never do apostleship and discipleship without prayer, the Holy Spirit and the word of God. Apostleship and discipleship is based on prayer, the Holy Spirit and the word of God. Luke 3:21-23, Jesus Christ after being baptized in water by John the Baptist, he prayed, then the heaven was open, the Holy Spirit came upon him like a dove and then God said this is my beloved son, whom I am well pleased, hear him. And after the water baptism Jesus was led by the Spirit to pray in the desert land (Luke 4:1-2). Jesus Christ sought God in the desert land with prayer and fasting. After that Prayer experience he was tempted by Satan three times and won by the word of God. And then the devil after finished his temptations he left him for a while. Luke 4:14-15 says this way:

*and Jesus returned in the power of the Spirit into Galilee: and there went out a fame of him through all the region round about. And he taught in their* synagogues, *being glorified of all.*

He was led to pray by the Holy Spirit, he sought God in prayer, and he was tempted by the enemy and won by the word of God, and returned in the power of the Spirit into Galilee. His fame went around in all the region and he taught the word of God in their synagogues being glorified by all people. Then the Lord Jesus Christ came to Nazareth where he was brought up and as his custom was he went into the synagogue and stood up to read. He found the place in the book of Isaiah these words (Luke 4:18-19):

*the Spirit of the Lord is upon me, because he hath anointed me to preach the gospel to the poor; he hath sent me to heal the brokenhearted, to preach deliverance to the captives, and recovering of sight to the blind, to set at* liberty *them that are bruised, To preach the acceptable year of the Lord.*

So as we have seen prayer, the Holy Spirit and the word of God was the basis of Jesus' apostleship and discipleship to Israel. Jesus Christ was a devoted man to God in prayer, the Holy Spirit and the word of God. Now throughout the book of Acts also prayer, the Holy Spirit and the word of God are mention before apostleship and discipleship. Let us see prayer, the Holy Spirit and the word of God in discipleship and apostleship in the book of Acts. In Acts chapter four when the apostles and disciples were threatened, they went to their own company and reported all that the chief priests and elders have said to them. When they heard that they lifted their voice to God in one accord. They prayed in Acts 4:29-31 this way:

*and now, Lord, behold their threatenings: and grant unto thy servants, that with all boldness they may speak thy word, by stretching forth thine hand to heal; and that signs and wonders may be done by the name of thy holy child Jesus. And when they had prayed, the place was shaken where they were assembled together; and they were all filled with the Holy Ghost, and they spake the word of God with boldness.*

Here in Acts chapter four we see prayer, the Holy Spirit and the word of God. The apostles and disciples first prayed, secondly they were filled with the Holy Spirit and thirdly they spoke the word of God with boldness. Acts 13:1-5, we see also prayer, the Holy Spirit and the word of God. Barnabas and Paul were successful in world apostleship and discipleship (Acts 13 -15) because of prayer, the Holy Spirit and the word of God. If you are going to be a successful disciple you need prayer, the Holy Spirit and the word of God. Disciples must pray. Have the Holy Spirit and follow his instructions and prioritise the word of God in everything they say and do. A disciple without prayer, the Holy Spirit and the word of God won't be a strong disciple but weak one. A disciple must have prayer lifestyle, see Colossians 4:2. A disciple must have the Spirit and follow him, see Colossians 1:8. And a disciple must have the word of God richly in his life, see Colossians 3:16.

## Discipleship and the glory of the Lord

Nevertheless when it shall turn to the Lord, the vail shall be taken away. Now the Lord is that Spirit: and where the Spirit of the Lord is, there is liberty. But we all, with open face beholding as in a glass the glory of the Lord, are changed into the same image from glory to glory, even as by the Spirit of the Lord.

### 2 Corinthians 3:16-18

The Holy Spirit is working in a life of a disciple. *Firstly*, if you turn to the Holy Spirit, he will take away the blindness on the word of God. *Secondly*, wherever the Holy Spirit is, he brings liberty. *And thirdly*, the Holy Spirit changes disciples into the same image of the glory of the Lord. These are three things the Holy Spirit does according to the Scripture above. The Holy Spirit is working on disciples to be like Christ and live according to the glory of the Lord. A disciple is a living epistle of Christ read with all people. The living epistles of Christ are not written with ink but by the Holy Spirit (2 Corinthians 3:2-3). As a disciple your life must not lose the image of the glory of the Lord. Your life is known and read by all people. Your life should be for the glory of the Lord and to magnify the Lord not wrong lifestyle. The Holy Spirit is upon your life to enable you live in the glory of the Lord. We are living in the days of glory, the Holy Spirit desire that you live according to the glory of the Lord. The Holy Spirit desires you to know the glory of the Lord. In the books of Luke and Acts, we see the Lord Jesus and the disciples served God and ministered in greater glory. The book of Acts is the fulfilment of the prophecy of Haggai. Haggai prophesied:

*The glory of this latter house shall be greater than of the former, saith the LORD of hosts: and in this place will I give peace, saith the LORD of hosts [Haggai 2:9].*

The church of Jesus Christ had the glory of the Lord so great in the book of Acts. But the glory of the last days' church and disciples shall be greater than the former. At the time of Haggai the prophet they were building the temple but it was nothing to them, compared to the former house. The first temple had so much glory than the temple in Haggai's time. The people of Israel had just arrived in their land and temple was in shame and useless. Haggai 2:3-5 says these words:

*Who is left among you that saw this house in her first glory? and how do ye see it now? is it not in your eyes in comparison of it as nothing? Yet now be strong, O Zerubbabel, saith the LORD; and be strong, O Joshua, son of Josedech, the high priest; and be strong, all ye people of the land, saith the LORD, and work: for I am with you, saith the* LORD *of hosts: according to the word that I covenanted with you when ye came out of* Egypt, *so my spirit remaineth among you: fear ye not.*

Glory is the work of the Holy Spirit. The Holy Spirit brings glory! No Holy Spirit, no glory. The presence and glory comes from the Holy Spirit. In Haggai's time, God said my Spirit remains among you; fear not. Glory cannot happen without the Holy Spirit. 1Peter 4:14 says the Spirit of glory and of God rests upon you. If you are going to experience glory it will be by the Holy Spirit. In the time of Eli's priest the glory departed from Israel (Ichabod), see 1 Samuel 4:21-22. But in King Solomon's time the glory (Shekinah) was displayed by the Holy Spirit in greatest level. The Holy Spirit displayed glory in unusual manner. The temple of King Solomon was filled with glory (2 Chronicles 5:13-14). Do you want the same glory and more, the answer is you need the Holy Spirit. The Holy Spirit wants you to know not only the goodness and grace of the Lord but also the glory of the Lord (Psalm 84:11). Do you want to see the Lord's goodness, grace and glory then you need the Holy Spirit. The Holy Spirit brings to the disciples not only the Lord's goodness and grace but also glory. If you want to see the glory and power of the Holy Spirit, you need to seek the Lord. King David shows us in Psalm 63:1-2, that the glory and power of the Holy Spirit comes by seeking the Lord. How do I seek the Lord? You seek the Lord through prayer and the word of God. Then and only then you can see the Holy Spirit in his presence and power. In the words of Scripture, Psalms 63:1-2 says:

*O* God, *thou art my God; early will I seek thee: my soul thirsteth for thee, my flesh longeth for thee in a dry and thirsty land, where no water is; to see thy power and thy glory, so as I have seen thee in the sanctuary.*

## Glory reference

Let us see the glory reference in the epistles. I have chosen 1 and 2 Corinthians to reveal glorious things in the word of God. You cannot know glory without the word of God and the Holy Spirit. If you want to know glory, ask the Holy Spirit to impart the glory upon you. Every disciple can experience the glory. Glory reference is found in;

1. 1 Corinthians 1:29, all glory belongs to God.

2. 1 Corinthians 2:7, the wisdom of God is ordained by God for our glory.

3. 1 Corinthians 2:8, Jesus Christ is the Lord of glory.

4.  1 Corinthians 3:21, do not boast on ministers of the gospel.

5.  1 Corinthians 5:6, don't boast on wrong lifestyle.

6.  1 Corinthians 9:15-16, boast not for what you do for the gospel and the work of the Lord.

7.  1 Corinthians 10:31, do all things for the glory of God.

8.  1 Corinthians 11:7, you are created in the image and glory of God.

9.  1 Corinthians 15:43, you will experience the Lord's glory and power after resurrection.

10. 2 Corinthians 1:20, the promise of God comes with the glory of God.

11. 2 Corinthians 3:8-9, the ministry of the Spirit is glorious.

12. 2 Corinthians 3:18 allow the Holy Spirit to transform you according to the image of the glory of the Lord.

13. 2 Corinthians 4:4, believe the glorious gospel of Christ.

14. 2 Corinthians 4:6, receive the insight of the Lord's glory.

15. 2 Corinthians 4:17, receive eternal weight of glory.

16. 2 Corinthians 5:12, boast not in appearance but in heart.

17. 2 Corinthians 8:19, minister grace to the glory of the Lord.

18. 2 Corinthians 8:23, be a messenger of the glory of Christ.

19. 2 Corinthians 10:16-18, boast in the Lord.

20. 2 Corinthians 11:12, don't boast on others, be yourself.

21. 2 Corinthians 12:1, it is not good to boast on how God uses you.

## Discipleship and ministry

And say to Archippus, Take heed to the ministry which thou hast received in the Lord, that thou fulfil it.

**Colossians 4:17**

Archippus was a disciple and he had a ministry but he was not doing anything with it for the Lord. Being idle and lazy is not good to the Lord. Or forsaking your ministry is not good for the Lord. The Lord wants you to be diligent disciple in the ministry. Don't be surprised I am speaking that a disciple must serve God in the ministry. You as a disciple, you have a ministry from the Lord. Archippus received ministry from the Lord. Just like the Lord has saved you, he has also given you a ministry. A disciple has two things: salvation and ministry from the Lord. Not just salvation, but salvation and ministry from the Lord. In Act 1:17,25, the disciples knew they had ministry before the Holy Spirit came upon them and received the power of God. A disciple must know he has a ministry. In fact the disciples knew three key words in serving the Lord: *witness, ministry and apostleship* (Acts 1:8,17,22,25). Then the Holy Spirit came upon them with power. The Holy Spirit empowered them to serve the Lord in the ministry and apostleship. A disciple is sent forth to serve God in the ministry in the church of the Lord. There are two more key Scriptures which prove a disciple has a ministry.

Scripture One: 1 Peter 4:10-11 says,

*As every man hath received the* gift, *even so minister the same one to another, as good stewards of the manifold grace of* God. *If any man speak, let him speak as the oracles of God; if any man minister, let him do it as of the ability which God giveth: that God in all things may be glorified through Jesus Christ, to whom be praise and dominion for ever and ever. Amen.*

Scripture Two: Ephesians 4:11-12 says,

*And he gave some, apostles; and some, prophets; and some, evangelists; and some,* pastors *and teachers; For the perfecting of the saints, for the work of the ministry, for the edifying of the* body of Christ:

In the Epistle of Peter, the apostle Peter said a disciple (you) have received a gift. A gift here is about ministry. You must know you have a ministry as the disciple of the Lord. The Lord wants you to serve him and minister in his church. In the Epistle of Ephesus, saints do the work of the ministry. Saints are disciples of the Lord. There are two types of ministries: the five ministry gifts and the ministry of saints or disciples. The five ministry gifts (verse eleven) their special tasks is the gospel and the work of the Lord. The five ministry gifts serve the Lord in world apostleship and perfecting the disciples to do the work of the ministry.

There are two purposes of the five ministry gifts (apostles, prophets, evangelists, pastors and teachers). *Purpose one*: to preach the gospel and do the work of the Lord. *Purpose two*: to perfect the saints for the work of the ministry. Now there are three questions, I think it will be good to answer them. *Question One*: who is a minister? A minister is a servant or one who serve the Lord. A minister is not only the five ministry gifts but also every disciple. According to Luke 1:2 and Acts 26:16, a disciple is a minister and a witness. Who is a witness? A witness is one who testifies the things he has seen and heard. *Question Two*: what is ministry? Ministry is service and God's work. Ministry is not just an organization or government department but service. The Lord wants you to serve as a disciple. *Question Three:* What is my ministry? Your ministry! Yes. You have a ministry as a disciple. This ministry is called the ministry of a disciple. You can know you ministry through prayer, the Holy Spirit and the word of God. One of the ways you can serve God nowadays is thought creational gifts of God listed in Romans 12:6-8. You can serve God in *prophecy, ministry, teaching, exhortation, giving, leadership and mercy.* The Scripture says these words:

*Having then gifts differing according to the grace that is given to us, whether prophecy, let us prophesy according to the proportion of faith; Or ministry, let us wait on our ministering: or he that teacheth, on teaching; Or he that exhorteth, on exhortation: he that giveth, let him do it with simplicity; he that ruleth, with diligence; he that sheweth mercy, with cheerfulness*

## Discipleship and moral standards

Giving no offence in anything, that the ministry be not blamed: But in all things approving ourselves as the ministers of God, in much patience, in afflictions, in necessities, in distresses,

**2 Corinthians 6:3-4**

The Lord has his moral standards. The Lord wants you to have ministerial ethics. If there something can bring down a ministry it is lack of ministerial ethics and sin. Sin in the ministry and church is a serious problem. The presence and power of the Lord can disappear if there is any form of sin. A disciple cannot afford to sin and at the same time serve the Lord. The Lord hates sin. When the Lord began to use you in the ministry be very careful with sin. Your ministry can go up or down based on the fact of purity and sin. Sin is one of the greatest weapons of Satan and the Devil (the archenemy of the Lord). Satan brings down a ministry or a minister through sin. What is sin? Sin is sin. There is no big sin and small sin. There is no great sin and little sin. There is no good sin and bad sin. When you sin, you cannot say, Satan made me do it. You are a free moral agent. As a person you have will, emotion and mind. Use your mind properly. According to the Holy Scripture, sin is defined as wrong doing, offence, rebellion, disobedience and spiritual wickedness. Sin is anything that fall short of the Lord's standards. The Lord in his word, commands his disciples not to sin. In the words of Scripture, 1 Corinthians 15:33-34 says these words:

*Be not deceived: evil communications corrupt good manners.*

*Awake to righteousness, and sin not; for some have not the knowledge of God: I speak this to your shame.*

Sin not, the Scripture says. If you know God you cannot sin. Sin brings shame. Sin is disgraceful act. Sin is immoral. Sin is opposite of the Lord's righteousness. There are people who teach and preach there is no sin in the world. That is a lie. Why then did the Lord Jesus come into the world? It was sin which made the Lord Jesus to die on the cross and suffer. There are people who say sin is not a big deal to God! That is a lie. God is against sin. Sin is serious offence to God. Sin is gross misconduct to God. God does not see or hear sin, and laugh. When a person sin; he faces the wrath and judgement of God. The only solution to the problem of sin is the Lord Jesus Christ. God forgives sin through the name of Jesus Christ, his Son. Now, let us discuss about three things: *pride, sex and money.* The Lord warns about pride, sex and money in the ministry. The Holy Scriptures are very clear concerning pride, sex and money. A person can sin against the Lord by pride, sex and money. What do you mean by pride? Pride is sin. Pride is evil. Pride spiritually speaking it is lack of humility and not being a humble person before God. Proverbs 8:11 says:

*The fear of the LORD is to hate evil: pride, and arrogancy, and the evil way, and the froward mouth, do I hate*

*Firstly, pride:* Cain lost the presence of God because of pride. Cain was angry when his offering was rejected by God. Cain had a sin of being disrespectful to God and he had no the fear of the Lord. After he killed his brother Abel, Cain talked to God and he had no fear, humility and repentance before the Lord God. His giving was refused by the Lord God because he did not do well. In the words of Scripture, Genesis 4:6-7 says: *and the LORD said unto Cain, Why art thou wroth? and why is thy countenance fallen? If thou doest well, shalt thou not be accepted? and if thou doest not well, sin lieth at the door. And unto thee shall be his desire, and thou shalt rule over him.* Pride is a worst sin and it can bring you down if you are not careful.

*Secondly, Sex*: what do you mean by sex? I am talking about sexual immorality. Any sex act outside marriage is sexual immorality. Any sex act outside marriage before and after is sin before God. Hebrews 13:4 says: *marriage is honourable in all, and the bed undefiled: but whoremongers and adulterers God will judge.* In the Holy Scripture perhaps the most anointed Judge in Israel was Samson. Samson had the power of the Spirit and was dynamically used by the Lord. But it came a time in his life he loved Delilah and lost the anointing of the Spirit. Samson did not know the Lord (the Holy Spirit) has departed from him and he was no longer a judge. In the words of Scripture, Judge 6:19-20 says: *and she made him sleep upon her* knees; *and she called for a man, and she caused him to shave off the seven locks of his head; and she began to afflict him, and his strength went from him. And she said, The Philistines be upon thee, Samson. And he awoke out of his sleep, and said, I will go out as at other times before, and shake myself. And he wist not that the LORD was departed from him.*

*Thirdly, money*: What do you mean by money? Money is not sin but the lust of money is a spiritual problem. The Holy Scriptures warns about abuse and misuse of money (lust of money, bribe, grid, theft or to love money than God). Money can bring you up or down depending on how you handle finance. The Lord Jesus had twelve disciples; one of them was called Judas Iscariot. Judas Iscariot was called, ordained and sent forth by the Lord to be an apostle but he sinned and betrayed the Lord Jesus by thirty pieces of silver (Shekels). In Acts chapter one, Peter and the rest of apostles had a meeting and voted, and they chose Matthias to replace Judas Iscariot. If you are not careful with sin, you will lose your ministry and cease to be a minister and God will chose a new person to replace you, which is the saddest thing in the world. In the words of Scripture, Acts 1:16-18 says: *men and brethren, this scripture must needs have been fulfilled, which the Holy Ghost by the mouth of David spake before concerning Judas, which was* guide *to them that took Jesus. For he was numbered with us, and had obtained part of this ministry. Now this man purchased a field with the* reward of iniquity; *and falling headlong, he burst asunder in the midst, and all his bowels gushed out.*

# CHAPTER 5
## Discipleship and World Apostleship

### Disciples do apostleship

But rise, and stand upon thy feet: for I have appeared unto thee for this purpose, to make thee a minister and a witness both of these things which thou hast seen, and of those things in the which I will appear unto thee; delivering thee from the people, and from the Gentiles, unto whom now I send thee, to open their eyes, and to turn them from darkness to light, and from the power of Satan unto God, that they may receive forgiveness of sins, and inheritance among them which are sanctified by faith that is in me

**Acts 26:16-18**

The key word for apostleship in the above Scripture is found in verse 17. The Lord Jesus said to Paul, unto whom now I *send* you. Apostleship is sending away for a specific work. Disciples do world apostleship. Disciples are prepared, trained and sent forth for world apostleship. Disciples know the gospel and work of the Lord (apostleship). Discipleship is connected to apostleship. You cannot separate the two. *What is discipleship? And what is world apostleship?* These are questions in people mind. In previous chapters I have covered the meaning of discipleship. For the sake of updating, let me repeat the simple meaning of discipleship again. More than preparation and training for ministry, discipleship is to be *a disciple of the Lord and able to make new disciples.* World apostleship simply means sending away for the gospel and the work of the Lord (ambassadorship to the world). In my book: *world apostleship*, I wrote the seven meaning of apostleship. Also I said, the word apostleship appears in the Holy Scripture four times. Let us find out where this word (apostleship) is written in the Holy Scriptures. The first time the word apostleship appears is Acts 1:25. In acts chapter one, apostleship is connected to witnessing and ministry. In fact in Luke 1:2, Luke wrote the apostles were eye-witnesses and ministers of the word. The second time the word apostleship appears is in Romans 1:5. In Romans chapter one, apostleship is connected with grace. In fact in Romans 15:15-16, Paul wrote boldly that by the grace of God he was made a minister of Jesus Christ; ministering the gospel of God. The third time apostleship appears is in 1 Corinthians 9:1-2. In this chapter nine of 1 Corinthians, apostleship is connected with the work of the Lord. Paul wrote the disciples at Corinth, that they are the seal of his apostleship in the Lord. And the fourth time apostleship is found in Galatians 2:8. Apostleship is connected to ancient and modern cultures. Peter was sent to people of Israel (the Jews) and Paul was sent to the people of the world (the Gentiles). In Romans 11:13, the apostle Paul said these words: *for I speak to you Gentiles, inasmuch as I am the apostle of the Gentiles, I magnify mine office.* Apostleship is specific. When God gives you apostleship, he sends you to a specific work. God sends ministers of the gospel and disciples to a specific group of people, culture, geographical region and generation. The Lord Jesus' apostleship was also specific. In Matthew 15:24, the Lord Jesus Christ said: *I am not sent but unto the lost sheep of the house of Israel.* Apostleship is a clear defined work and specific work of God to a group of people or culture or region or generation and century. Now let us learn the seven meaning of the word apostleship.

The seven meaning of world apostleship are as follows:

1. Sent away by the Lord Jesus Christ with a purpose in the world, Acts 26:16-18.

2. Taking the Name of Jesus Christ to the world and advance work, Acts 15:25-26.

3. Taking the gospel and work of God to the world, Acts 13:2,4-5 and Acts 14:1-4,21,26

4. Holy Spirit new venture for every person, Acts 16:6-10 and Acts 22:21

5. World service (to turn people from idols to serve God), 1 Thessalonians 1:8-9

6. Ambassadorship of the gospel and discipleship, Acts 19:1-10 and Ephesians 6:19-20

7. The authority and commission of Jesus Christ, Mark 16:15-20 and Romans 1:1-2

## Apostleship: called, ordained and sent forth

And he goeth up into a mountain, and calleth unto him whom he would: and they came unto him. And he ordained twelve, that they should be with him, and that he might send them forth to preach, And to have power to heal sicknesses, and to cast out devils

**Mark 3:13-15**

To understand apostleship, you need to see certain words in the Scripture above. The words are and *call* unto him whom he would, he *ordained* and that he might *send them forth.* Those words you just read are about apostleship. Apostleship begins with seeking God. The Scripture says: the Lord Jesus went up into the mountain, to do what? To seek God in prayer and he found him. When the Lord Jesus came down from the mountain of God, he had all the answers in the world, who and who should be in the list for the work of apostleship. Now, the word ordained, I don't mean for a second, that every person who is ordained, is called and sent forth for apostleship by the Lord. And I don't mean either that to do apostleship you must be ordained. Apostleship is divine call. The word ordained is used so much in our modern generation, others abuse and misuse it. While other people use it properly according to the word of God and the Holy Spirit. In his work and apostleship to the Gentiles (none Jewish people), Paul the apostle said that he is ordained and appointed by the Lord. Apostleship is to be ordained and appointed by the Lord and for the gospel sake.

Scripture one: 1 Timothy 2:7 says, *whereunto I am ordained a preacher, and an apostle, (I speak the truth in* Christ, *and lie not;) a teacher of the Gentiles in faith and verity.*

Scripture two: 2 Timothy 1:11 says, w*hereunto I am appointed a preacher, and an apostle, and a teacher of the Gentiles.*

What is to ordain? And what is to appoint? The answers to these two questions will help you to understand apostleship. To ordain means to set apart for the Lord's use or put forth. To appoint means to assign for specific task. Therefore apostleship is to be set apart for the Lord's use and to be assigned for specific task. Paul was set apart and assigned by the Lord to be *a preacher, an apostle and a teacher* of the Gentiles in faith and truth. Going back to the twelve disciples, they were called, ordained and sent forth by the Lord. Putting the word ordained in the right use, we can say, they were called, set apart for the Lord's use and sent forth.

## Discipleship, impartation and apostleship

And he called unto him the twelve, and began to send them forth by two and two; and gave them power over unclean spirits

**Mark 6:7**

In the gospel and work of the Lord there three special words: *discipleship, impartation and apostleship.* The Lord Jesus trained disciples, imparted power to them and sent them away in the streets to do apostleship. The twelve disciples were called first disciples of the Lord and then sent out for apostleship. In their earlier mission and apostleship to Israel, the twelve disciples were called by the Lord, given power and sent forth two by two. In the Scripture above, I want you to see three special words: call, send forth and give power. *Special word one*: call. The disciples were called unto the Lord. The Scripture says, and he called unto him the twelve. Here we find our special word one: discipleship. Discipleship is a call unto the Lord or the Lord's call. You cannot be a disciple by yourself; you must receive the call of the Lord Jesus Christ. Discipleship is a divine call. *Special word two:* give power. The Scripture says, Lord gave them power. What power? Power is the anointing for service. Here we find our second special word: impartation. The Lord probably laid his hands upon them since in the Scripture that is symbolic of impartation. Another ways of doing special impartation are by the word of God and the Holy Spirit (John 3:34 and John 20:21-23). *Special word three*: send forth. The Scripture says, and began to send them forth by two and two. Here we find our third special word: apostleship. Apostleship is the third special word and greatest word than all other special words of discipleship and impartation. Apostleship includes preaching the gospel with healing and miracles. The twelve disciples went out and preached that men should repent (the gospel). And they casted out many devils and anointed with oil many who were sick, and healed them. That is doing healing and miracles. *Notice:* the twelve disciples did not anoint people bound by devils but the anointed the sick and healed them. How did they deal with the devils? They casted them out in Jesus' name. You too can do the same and so much more, in 21$^{st}$ century and modern culture.

Mark 6:12-13 says: *and they went out, and preached that men should repent. And they cast out many devils, and anointed with oil many that were sick, and healed them.*

And today by the word of God and the Holy Spirit, the Lord Jesus Christ has sent us forth for mission and world apostleship. Just like, the disciples went out and preached the gospel with healing and miracles, the same way the Lord Jesus has called and sent us forth. Is world apostleship for today? Yes. Can anybody do world apostleship? Yes. What places can you do world apostleship? Anywhere in the world, where Christ is unnamed, the gospel is unknown and the work of the Lord is not established and increasing. Does God recognize world apostleship today? Yes. Is world apostleship known and acknowledged by most people? Yes. We thank God although in years back many fought the term "apostleship" but now the Holy Spirit has opened people's eyes and ears in regard to the gospel and work of the Lord. In Mark 16:15,20, the Lord Jesus gave commission and authority to his twelve disciples. In Mark 6:7,12-13, the twelve disciples did have earlier mission and apostleship in the streets of Israel for a short time. But now, the Lord Jesus Christ sent them forth to every creature in the world. The Lord Jesus spoke the most gracious and glorious words. Other people call these words the Great Commission; to some people these words are the Lord's instructions and the Last words of the Master. Read on, here are the words of Scripture for the work of apostleship, the Lord said:

*And he said unto them, Go ye into all the world, and preach the gospel to every creature. And they went forth, and preached every where, the Lord working with them, and confirming the word with signs following. Amen*

A to Z of Personal Discipleship

These key points of will help you to understand personal discipleship. These are points from the Holy Bible and will help you find and follow the Lord Jesus Christ. Each alphabet letter stands for a biblical truth that you have to understand and be a good disciple of the Lord Jesus Christ.

A.     A is for apostleship, see Acts 1:15,25. Disciples do world apostleship. Disciples are prepared, trained and sent forth for world apostleship. Disciples know the gospel and work of the Lord (apostleship). Discipleship is connected to apostleship.

B.     B is for boldness, see Acts 4:13. The Lord Jesus Christ makes the difference in life. If you received the Lord Jesus Christ as your Saviour, you are made a new person and totally different with an average person.

C.     C is for Christianity, see Acts 11:26. When the Scripture says: the disciples were first called Christians that means they were saved and had Christ likeness. There was a difference of lifestyle between Christians and Pagan people. A disciple resembles Christ his Lord, Master and Teacher.

D.     D is for Devotion, see Acts 6:4. A disciple is devoted in prayer and the word of God. Discipleship is strengthened by prayer and the word of God. A disciple seeks God and studies the word of God. A disciple is devoted to the Lord by prayer and the word.

E.     E is for eternal life; see Acts 13:46 and John 3:16. Discipleship is linked with eternal life. A disciple has eternal life. One of the tasks of the disciple is to share with all people the eternal life of the Lord God.

F.     F is for Faith in Christ, see Acts 24:24-25 and Hebrew 12:2. Discipleship is adherence to the Lord and Master's faith. The Lord Jesus Christ is author and finisher of his disciple's faith. A disciple has faith in his Lord and Master.

G.     G is for Growth, see Acts 6:1-2. Notice the number of the disciples of the Lord was multiplied. The disciples of the Lord grew so much to the extent Luke called the large number of disciples. The number of disciples grew in number then, and must grow in number today.

H.     H is for Heaven, see 2 Peter 3:13. A disciple has two clear goals: to go to heaven and while on the earth live for the Lord, and do the work of the Lord and spread the gospel. A disciple set goals and achieve them in the Lord.

I.     I is for Impact, see Acts 4:33. The glorious thing of a disciple is impact. The Scripture says with great power the apostles gave witness of the resurrection of the Lord and great grace was upon them all. A disciple makes impact wherever he goes for the Lord.

J.     J is for justification, see Romans 8:29-30. A disciple not only is predestined and called by God but also justified and glorified. A disciple is destined and called for the glory of the Lord. A disciple belongs to the eternal glory of God.

K.     K is for kingdom, see Romans 14:17. Disciples are kings and priests in the kingdom of God. According to the Epistle of Peter (1 Peter 2:9-10), disciples are chosen generation, a royal priesthood, a holy nation and peculiar people.

L.      L is for the Lord, John 13:13-14. Jesus Christ is Lord and Master to all disciples. When you are saved, Jesus Christ is now your Lord and Master. The Lord Jesus Christ desires his disciples to follow his example and serve one another.

M.      M is for Ministry, Colossians 4:17. A disciple has a ministry. In the book of Acts, there were disciples *who minister in power* to Apostle Paul when he was half dead. And Paul was rescued from danger of his life. A disciple has received a ministry from the Lord.

N.      N is for New Testament, 1 Corinthians 11:23-26. Discipleship is a New Testament thing. The Lord Jesus Christ desires new disciples to be made in the New Testament. God has made new covenant with the disciples through Jesus Christ.

O.      O is for One Accord, Acts 15:25-26. The secret of success of the disciples in the book of acts was one accord. And because of one accord, the Lord gave them success and favour in their work and apostleship to the world.

P.      P is for power, see Luke 24:48-49 and Acts 1:8. A disciple is a powerful witness. A disciple is anointed with the Holy Spirit and power of God. A disciple is not weak but strong in the Lord and his power.

Q.      Q is for Quality and Quantity, Acts 6:1-3. Discipleship is not about only making many disciples with no quality whatsoever. Discipleship is about both quality and quantity. Disciples are many in the Lord and good in the Lord.

R.      R is for reported well, see Acts 16:1-3. Before Paul the apostle chose and took Timothy to his work and apostleship to the world. Timothy was reported well by the brethren. A disciple has a good report.

S.      S is for salvation and healing of others, see Acts 4:10-12. Peter the apostle said the name of Jesus Christ heals and saves. This was after a notable miracle of the lame man. A disciple takes salvation and healing of the Lord to other people.

T.      T is for Training, see Luke 6:12-13. The Lord Jesus Christ for three years trained and prepared the disciples to preach the gospel and do the work of the Lord (apostleship). A disciple is trained and prepared by the Lord before his work and the gospel.

U.      U is for understanding the Holy Bible, see Luke 24:44-45 and 2 Timothy 3:15-17. The Lord Jesus Christ gives understand to the disciples for the word of God through the Holy Spirit. The Holy Spirit is the breath of God.

V.      V is for vessel unto honour, see 2 Timothy 2:20-21. A disciple is not only a follower of the Lord but he is a vessel unto the Lord and Master Jesus Christ. A disciple is for the service of the Lord. The Lord uses a disciple to serve him and minister in the church.

W.      W is for Witness, see Acts 23:11 and 2 Timothy 2:2. The Lord stands with his disciples. The Lord speaks to his disciples to testify him and witness the gospel in other parts of the world. Witnessing is part of discipleship. A disciple is a witness of Jesus Christ.

X.      X is for Expansion Acts 16:4-5. Discipleship is about being established in the faith and increased in number. God has purposed that discipleship should expand both spiritually and numerically. The Lord wants disciples to move forward not backward.

Y.      Y is for Yes to apostleship of Lord, 1 Corinthians 9:1-2. Apostleship is about the gospel and people of the Lord. Apostleship must go global and be financed to the parts of the world where Christ is unnamed, the gospel is unknown and his work has not grown and expanded.

Z.      Z is for A to Z. The Lord Jesus Christ is A to Z of personal discipleship. The Lord Jesus Christ is the one who call people to be disciples and give them special task to make new disciples and teach them all the commandment of the Lord.

## Discipleship and prophecy

And in these days came prophets from Jerusalem unto Antioch. And there stood up one of them named Agabus, and signified by the Spirit that there should be great dearth throughout all the world: which came to pass in the days of Claudius Caesar. Then the disciples, every man according to his ability, determined to send relief unto the brethren which dwelt in Judaea

**Acts 11:28-29**

Signify by the Spirit! What is that? To signify by the Spirit means to show forth by the Holy Spirit. Jesus when teaching about the Holy Spirit, he said: when the Spirit shall come he will lead you into all truth and he shall speak *the things to come.* In the Scripture above it is fulfilment of the words which Jesus taught. The Holy Spirit speaks and works by prophecy. There are places where prophecy is not taken serious. There are places prophecy is misused and abused. We need to understand two facts: one, not all prophecies are false. Two, not all prophecies are true. Thus why, it is important to hear "*this is what says the Holy Spirit*" from a person with proven ministry like Agabus. Agabus was a well known, nurtured and matured prophet. He would not say something the Holy Spirit is not saying or doing. Agabus was a senior prophet with a company of prophets. Another three points I want to make are: *point one*, is disciples pay attention to prophecy and act accordingly. When Agabus prophesied the disciples heard attentively and acted. The Scripture says: Then the disciples, every man according to his ability, determined to send relief unto the brethren which dwelt in Judaea. They disciples did not throw away the prophecy but they acted immediately. *Point two*: the Holy Spirit uses disciples to give prophecy to a minister or Christian. Acts 21:4 says: *and finding disciples, we tarried there seven days: who said to Paul through the Spirit, that he should not go up to Jerusalem.* The disciples prophesied by the Spirit and warned Paul not to go to Jerusalem city. *The third point*, I want to make is prophets and prophecy is not about controlling people's will, emotion and mind. If a person received the prophecies of the Lord and do nothing it is up to them and their God. After the giving of prophecy all things are in the hands of God. Consider these words of God to Ezekiel the prophet. In Ezekiel 3:16-18, God said:

*And it came to pass at the end of seven days, that the word of the LORD came unto me, saying, Son of man, I have made thee a watchman unto the house of Israel: therefore hear the word at my mouth, and give them warning from me. When I say unto the wicked, Thou shalt surely die; and thou givest him not warning, nor speakest to warn the wicked from his wicked way, to save his life; the same wicked man shall die in his iniquity; but his blood will I require at thine hand. Yet if thou warn the wicked, and he turn not from his wickedness, nor from his wicked way, he shall die in his iniquity; but thou hast delivered thy soul*

Disciples of today need to speak not half truth but to declare all the counsel of God to the lost and found people of God (Acts 20:26-27). Disciples must be faithful to speak both the word of God and the word of the Lord (prophetic word). And once you have delivered the prophecy of the Lord leave the matter in the hands of God. Your responsibility as a disciple is also to act on the prophetic word when you hear it. We are living in a generation where so much have been preached and taught but less has been done. Our generation is not different with prophet Ezekiel's generation. The people appear as the Lord's people but do nothing at all, after they hear the prophetic word. And God was not pleased with such behaviour. God said to Ezekiel, the people are not honest; they don't do your words. In Ezekiel 33:31-33, God said:

*And they come unto thee as the people cometh, and they sit before thee as my people, and they hear thy words, but they will not do them: for with their mouth they shew much love, but their heart goeth after their covetousness. And, lo, thou art unto them as a very lovely* song *of one that hath a* pleasant voice, *and can play well on an instrument: for they hear thy words, but they do them not. And when this cometh to pass, (lo, it will come,) then shall they know that a prophet hath been among them*

## The seven fold prophecies of the Lord

When you do what God is saying and the Lord's people do not act accordingly, the word of the Lord will do God's will and accomplish his purpose on earth. The prophetic word will fulfil the divine cause and the Lord's people shall surely know you were sent and set forth by the Holy Spirit. Only do not increase or decrease the word of the Lord. As a disciple declare all the counsel of God. Finally, I would like to declare to you the seven prophecies of the Lord to all modern disciples of Jesus Christ. The seven prophecies of the Lord from are:

1. Prophecy one. The Spirit says: spiritual difficulties ahead, stay away from people who have wrong motives to harm the Lord's flock and inheritance. See, Acts 20:29-30. Watch and pray, and abide in my word. Respect the true leaders I have put over you.

2. Prophecy two. The Spirit says: very words of God are precious. Do not throw away the sound words. I have written in the Holy Bible sound words; take

them seriously. Keep my sound words to you. See, 2 Timothy 1:13

3.  Prophecy three. The Spirit says: that good thing which was committed to you, keep by the Holy Spirit who dwells in us. Keep your faith, ran the race set forth ahead of you. Finish your course with joy. See, 2 Timothy 1:14

4.  Prophecy four: The Spirit says: do not deny my power. Live in godliness. Turn away from such people who say one thing and do another thing. Seek the Lord and he will make you a strong disciple. See, 2 Timothy 3:5

5.  Prophecy five. The Spirit says: stir up the gift of salvation, the Holy Spirit and ministry in you. I have called you to do gracious and glorious things in life. So rise up for the Lord. See, 2 Timothy 1:5-7.

6.  Prophecy six. The Spirit says: live with a pure heart. Do not have an evil heart which does nor please the Lord. But as a disciple follow righteousness, faith, charity, peace, with them that call on the Lord out of a pure heart. See, 2 Timothy 2:22

7.  Prophecy seven. The Spirit says: but foolish and unlearned questions avoid, knowing that they do gender strifes. And the servant of the Lord must not strive; but be gentle unto all men, apt to teach, patient. See, 2 Timothy 2:23-24

## Discipleship, the Holy Spirit and you

And it came to pass, that, while Apollos was at Corinth, Paul having passed through the upper coasts came to Ephesus: and finding certain disciples. He said unto them, Have ye received the Holy Ghost since ye believed? And they said unto him, We have not so much as heard whether there be any Holy Ghost.

**Acts 19:1-2**

Discipleship has to do with both finding disciples and making disciples. If you find disciples who lack spiritual things of the word of God and the Holy Spirit, you make sure they receive as the Lord commanded. This was the case here in Acts 19. Paul came to Ephesus and found twelve disciples there who knew not the Holy Spirit and have not received the Holy Spirit. Paul taught them about the Holy Spirit and prayed for them to receive the Holy Spirit. Notice: the Holy Spirit come upon you in respond to the word of God and prayer you made to the Lord. Acts 19:6-7 says: *and when Paul had laid his hands upon them, the Holy Ghost came on them; and they spake with tongues, and prophesied. And all the men were about twelve.* Do not be surprised these twelve men spoke with tongues and prophesied! When the Holy Spirit comes upon you such results of tongues and prophecies do happen. What happen when the Holy Spirit comes upon you? You receive power and speak with tongues. In the Scripture above, they spoke with tongues and prophesied, we don't see power here. But according to the teaching of the Lord Jesus, he said three things will happen: *the Holy Spirit, power and tongues.* In Mark 16:17 and Acts 1:8, the

Lord Jesus spoke on the Holy Spirit, power and tongues. Paul the apostle who received the Holy Spirit in Act 9:15-19, spoke also on the Holy Spirit, power and tongues. In 1 Corinthians 2:4-5, Paul said about demonstration of the Holy Spirit and power. And in 1 Corinthians 14:18, Paul said he spoke with tongues than the disciples at Corinth. The Lord Jesus Christ taught about the gift and promise of the Holy Spirit in Luke 11:11-13 and Acts 1:4-5. **Who is this Holy Spirit?** The Holy Spirit is a person, gift, promise and co-worker (partner). The Holy Spirit is the gift and promise of the Father. Can I receive the Holy Spirit? Yes. Can receive power? Yes. Can I speak with tongues? Yes. A disciple must receive the Holy Spirit. The Holy Spirit deals with disciples. You cannot be a disciple without the Holy Spirit. To be a disciple and make disciples you need the Holy Spirit. How do I know I have receive the Holy Spirit? You know you have the Holy Spirit, *firstly* by faith (Galatians 3:2-3,5), *secondly*, by the fruit of the Spirit (Galatians 5:22-23). *Thirdly*, by the word of God (2 Timothy 1:14). *Fourthly*, by your life being transformed (Acts 9:17-19). *And fifthly*, by speaking in tongues (Acts 19:6-7). If you know the person and work of the Holy Spirit, you will understand that discipleship also is the work of the Holy Spirit. The Holy Spirit wants to touch the disciples. The Holy Spirit desires you. The Holy Spirit speaks and works in the life of disciples. Acts 13:2,4-5,47 and Acts 14:1-3,21,26 show that apostleship and discipleship are the work of the Holy Spirit. The Holy Spirit is for sure at work on apostleship and discipleship. The Holy Spirit calls, empowers and sends forth people for world apostleship and discipleship. When the Holy Spirit is at work on apostleship and discipleship there are *seven results*. The seven results of

Benjamin Maira

the Holy Spirit are found in Acts 14:1-28. The seven results of the Holy Spirit for apostleship and discipleship are as follows:

1. Great multitude are saved, Acts 14:1
2. Signs, wonders and healing are done, Acts 14:3,8-10
3. Disciples make impact, Acts 14:19-20
4. New disciples are made, Acts 14:21
5. Souls of disciples are confirmed (strengthened), Acts 14:22
6. Work success is achieved at the top level, Acts 14:26
7. Disciples are gathered together, Acts 14:27-28

## Discipleship and the Local church

And thence sailed to Antioch, from whence they had been recommended to the grace of God for the work which they fulfilled. And when they were come, and had gathered the church together, they rehearsed all that God had done with them, and how he had opened the door of faith unto the Gentiles. And there they abode long time with the disciples

**Acts 14:26-28**

The Antioch church is a real church model to follow in our generation. There are five activities of a local church and that the Antioch church had. What are church activities? The church activities are *world apostleship, personal discipleship,*

*public worship, group fellowship and financial stewardship.*
Every local church must be doing these five activities of the
local church. Let us deal with discipleship from Acts 11:25-
26 and Acts 14:26-28. Acts 11:25-26 was before Barnabas
and Paul were sent forth by the church and the Holy Spirit
for world apostleship. At the church of the Lord, we see
Barnabas and Paul, assembled the Antioch church and
taught the many people for the whole year, and disciples
were first called Christians. Disciples need the impact of
the word of God in their lives. Disciples need to know
and acknowledge the word of God is powerful. There are
two Scriptures which Paul showed how the word of God is
powerful.

Scripture one: 1 Thessalonians 2:13 says, *For this cause also*
*thank we* God *without ceasing, because, when ye received the*
*word of God which ye heard of us, ye received it not as the word*
*of men, but as it is in truth, the word of God, which effectually*
*worketh also in you that believe.*

Scripture two: 2 Timothy 2:9 says: *Wherein I suffer trouble,*
*as an evil doer, even unto bonds; but the word of God is not*
*bound.*

The word of God works in you effectively. The word of God
also is not bound. The Holy Spirit speaks and works by the
word of God. Now, concerning discipleship in Acts 14:26-
28, we see Barnabas and Paul after their world apostleship,
they went back to Antioch and gathered together the church,
and they rehearsed all that God had done with them. The
disciples heard the report of the gospel and work of the Lord.
After that Paul and Barnabas abode along time with the

disciples. Discipleship was a strong activity at the Antioch church. Not only discipleship was a strong activity in the Antioch church but also apostleship, worship, fellowship and stewardship. The Antioch church way of doing church is one of the church models to follow. Now let us see full explanation of each activity at the Antioch church. The five church activities are:

1.  **World Apostleship:** Acts 13:4-5,46-47, Barnabas and Paul called, empowered and sent forth by the Holy Spirit for world apostleship. The Antioch church is known as the sending church. World Apostleship is about the gospel and the work of the Lord to the world. The Holy Spirit wants us to do both world apostleship and discipleship. The Holy Spirit wants you to be strong in world apostleship.

2.  **Personal Discipleship:** Acts 11:25-26 and Acts 14:26-28, the Antioch church was strong in personal discipleship. Disciples were taught the word of God and transformed to Christ likeness. Disciples also were gathered together and receive report of the gospel and work of the Lord (apostleship). The Holy Spirit wants you to be strong in personal discipleship.

3.  **Public Worship:** Acts 13:2. When the scripture says, they ministered unto the Lord that is worship. The Antioch church was a church with strong atmosphere of public worship. Worship and seeking the Lord releases you to you divine call. Barnabas and Paul could have stayed in Antioch and never fulfilled their divine call had not been

worship and the Holy Spirit instruction. The Holy Spirit wants you to be strong in public worship.

4. **Group Fellowship:** Acts 15:30-31. Barnabas and Paul gathered together the disciples and delivered to them the Epistle (written message). The disciples were consoled by the word of God and the Holy Spirit. The Holy Spirit speaks and works in times of group fellowship. The church must practice highly fellowship of disciples. A disciple must fellowship with other disciples at the local church. The Holy Spirit wants you to be strong in group fellowship.

5. **Financial Stewardship:** Acts 11:28-29. Barnabas and Paul were used by the Lord in financial stewardship. Financial stewardship is giving. The disciples must practice financial giving. Giving to the Lord and the gospel work is very significant. Disciples must know financial giving opens doors, bring promotion and releases favour. The Holy Spirit wants you to be strong in financial stewardship.

# EPILOGUE

Ministry Scripture:

Above all remember these verses of the books of Acts 16:1-3 and Acts 26:16-18 below. The Lord Jesus Christ appeared to Apostle Paul and said to him: I have appeared to this purpose, to make you a minister and witness both of these things which you has seen, and of those things in which I will appear unto thee; delivering thee from the people, and from the Gentiles, unto whom now I *send* thee. The term send is Apostleship. The term purpose means apostleship is special task and the Lord had a reason or intention why he appeared to Paul. The Lord Jesus Christ appeared to Paul with one purpose, to make him a minister and witness of the things he has heard and seen now and the things the Lord will show him in the future.

Let this ministry scripture from the book of Acts 16:1-3 and Acts 26:16-18 imparts to you to speak the gospel and do the work of the work of the Lord. May you worship and serve the Lord Jesus Christ in a special way. This is the key scripture for world apostleship and discipleship. It is my desire God to open doors to you so that you experience top level of world apostleship and discipleship in our modern cultures and 21st century. In the book of Acts 26:16-18, the Lord Jesus Christ spoke of apostleship (now I send you). In the book of Acts 16:1-3, Paul the apostle found a well reported disciple named Timothy and took him for training and mentored him that is discipleship. World Apostleship and Discipleship are connected together. The Lord wants us to do both in this world. The Lord Jesus Christ himself did *apostleship and discipleship* in Israel according to the book of Luke.

Acts 16:1-3 says:

Then came he to Derbe and Lystra: and, behold, a certain *disciple* was there, named Timotheus, the son of a certain woman, which was a Jewess, and *believed*; but his father was a Greek: which was *well reported of by the brethren* that were at Lystra and Iconium. Him would Paul have *to go forth with him*; and took and circumcised him because of the Jews which were in those quarters: for they knew all that his father was a Greek.

Acts 26:16-18 says:

But rise, and stand upon thy feet: for I have appeared unto thee for this *purpose, to make thee a minister and a witness* both *of these things* which thou hast seen, and *of those things* in the which *I will appear* unto thee; *delivering thee* from the people, and from the Gentiles, *unto whom now I send thee, to open their eyes, and to turn* them from darkness to light, and from the power of Satan unto God, that they may *receive* forgiveness of sins, and inheritance among them which are *sanctified by faith that is in me.*

# MINISTRY NOTES

## Chapter 1

Discipleship Today

Modern disciples

Disciples were first called Christians (Acts 11:25-26). What does that mean? It means disciples were identified with the Lord Jesus Christ. Christians are people belong to Christ. Or people who have Christ likeness. It is like in Acts 4:13, when they saw the boldness of Peter and John, and perceived they were unlearned and ignorant they took the knowledge of them that they had been with Jesus. What made difference in Peter and John was Jesus' discipleship in their life. In other words it was the teaching of Jesus Christ and the Holy Spirit touch. And here at the Antioch church the disciples were transformed because of the teaching of the word of God and the Holy Spirit touch. Barnabas and Paul taught much people in the church for the whole year. Discipleship makes impact. And thus is why discipleship is very important to people today. If we are going to impact the world today we need discipleship. In his ministry and apostleship, Jesus did also discipleship. The apostles, all of them were involved in the gospel and work of the Lord but also in discipleship. Discipleship does not only mean training for ministry. Discipleship has deeper meaning than that. Even in Jesus time, discipleship was not limited to training for ministry but also discipleship meant to find Christ the Lord and follow him. Or discipleship was meant the call of Christ to know him and follow him. Discipleship is a life of dedication. Discipleship is lifetime devotion to the Lord Jesus Christ. Discipleship is not only three years commitment to a school of ministry until you graduate for ministry.

## Chapter 2

Discipleship and Impartation

Impartation for disciples

This is how Paul and Barnabas became disciples. Paul and Barnabas were saved in different time and places but the Lord brought them together for world apostleship. But before world apostleship Barnabas trained and cared for Paul in the church of the Lord until the day the Holy Spirit sent them away for world apostleship. There are three key words you need to understand: *discipleship, impartation and apostleship*. Barnabas and Paul were first made disciples, then received impartation and sent away for the greatest thing of all: apostleship. In Acts 13:1-2, when all ministers sought the Holy Spirit and ministered to the Lord, we see three things call, impartation and send. When other ministers laid their hands on Barnabas and Paul that was *impartation*. What impartation? It is the impartation of grace and power for

God's service. Or in others words it was the impartation of favour and the anointing. We know this from Paul's Epistle to the Romans. In Romans 15:15-19, Paul said he was made a minister of Jesus Christ by grace and he did signs and wonders by the power of the Spirit of God. Where did he receive grace and power? He received grace and power from impartation service at the Antioch church. To be a disciple you need special impartation of grace and power. Also in the book of Ephesus 3:5-7, Paul wrote about the grace and power of God. Paul said he was made a minister of the gospel by the gift of God's grace according to the effectual working of his power. A disciple cannot do world apostleship or the gospel and work of the Lord without grace and power. You need God's impartation upon you. You need grace and power for what God has called you to be and do.

## Chapter 3

The Holy Spirit and Discipleship

Disciples with touch

The Holy Spirit touches the disciples in different ways. In Acts 13:52 the disciples were filled with joy and the Holy Spirit. Notice: the disciples were *filled* with *joy* and with *the Holy Spirit*. You need both joy and the Holy Spirit. Not just joy but the Holy Spirit also. Both in Old Testament and New Testament we see joy and the Holy Spirit. The Holy Spirit touched people in both Testaments: Old and New. The Holy Spirit touches people by his presence and power. The book of Acts and the Epistles are the evidence of the presence and power of the Holy Spirit. The results of the presence of the Holy Spirit are: **firstly**, the touch of God. The presence brings the touch of God. **Secondly**, the presence releases the voice of God. The presence makes people sensitive to the voice of God. **Thirdly**, the presence releases the power of God. The presence is the key to the power of God. Time spent in the presence of God is not time wasted. **Fourthly**, the presence brings the character of God. The Bible says this character of God is the fruit of the Spirit (Galatians 5:22-23). **Fifthly,** the presence brings the call of God. The Holy Spirit calls people while they are in the presence of God. The good example of this point is Acts 13:2. The presence of the Holy Spirit is so important. When the Holy Spirit enters your life, these five things will happen in your life.

## Chapter 4

Discipleship and Good Report

Disciples are well reported

Paul found Timothy and took him to go forth with him. Certain things are mentioned of Timothy. He was a disciple, a believer and well reported. Paul must have been pleased to hear good report of Timothy. A good report is a good thing to a disciple. A good report brings divine connection with sound ministers of the gospel. A disciple must be a believer with good report before the Lord and the brethren. A disciple as we have seen in New Testament is not just a student but a believer with good report. If Timothy was not a believer and with good report; Paul could not take him and go forth with him in the gospel and work of the Lord.

How you conduct yourself before the Lord and the brethren is very important. Discipleship is the Lord's call. Good report is about good character. Timothy had both. so many people have the Lord's call but lack good character. You find disciples with the Lord's call but with bad character. You need to have both the Lord's call and good character. Character is everything. Everywhere you go character is highly required (good report). In the first early church in Jerusalem the apostles wanted seven men to do hospitality and helping of the poor saints. Peter the apostle gave a list of three things required: *a good report, the Holy Spirit and wisdom.* You see good report is required everywhere you go. In the words of Scripture, Acts 6:3 says: *wherefore, brethren, look ye out among you seven men of honest report, full of the Holy Ghost and* wisdom, *whom we may appoint over this business.* Every disciple need to have good report, full of the Holy Spirit and wisdom. Did Timothy have all three things: good report, the Holy Spirit and wisdom? The answer is yes. Acts 16:2 says Timothy was well reported of by the brethren. 2 Timothy 1:14 says Timothy had the Holy Spirit. And 2 Timothy 3:15 says that the Scriptures which Timothy have known since he was a child are able to make him wise.

## Chapter 5

Discipleship and World Apostleship

Disciples do apostleship

The key word for apostleship in Acts 26:16-18 is found in verse 17. The Lord Jesus said to Paul, unto whom now I *send* you. Apostleship is sending away for a specific work.

Disciples do world apostleship today. Disciples are trained, ordained and sent forth for world apostleship. Disciples know the gospel and work of the Lord (apostleship). Discipleship is connected to apostleship. You cannot separate the two. *What is discipleship? And what is world apostleship?* These are questions in people mind. In previous chapters I have covered the meaning of discipleship. For the sake of updating, let me repeat the simple meaning of discipleship again. More than preparation and training for ministry, discipleship is to be *a disciple of the Lord and make new disciples*. World apostleship simply means sending away for the gospel and the work of the Lord (ambassadorship to the world). In my book: *world apostleship*, I wrote the seven meaning of apostleship. Also I said the word apostleship appears in the Holy Scripture four times. Let us find out where this word (apostleship) is written in the Holy Scriptures. The word apostleship appears in the Bible four times. The first time the word apostleship appears is Acts 1:25. In acts chapter one, apostleship is connected to witnessing and ministry. In fact in Luke 1:2, Luke wrote the apostles were eye-witnesses and ministers of the word. The second time the word apostleship appears is in Romans 1:5. In Romans chapter one, apostleship is connected with grace. In fact in Romans 15:15-16, Paul wrote boldly that by the grace of God he was made a minister of Jesus Christ; ministering the gospel of God. The third time apostleship appears is in 1 Corinthians 9:1-2. In this chapter nine of 1 Corinthians, apostleship is connected with the work of the Lord. Paul wrote the disciples at Corinth are the seal of his apostleship in the Lord. And the fourth time apostleship is found in Galatians 2:8. Apostleship is connected to ancient and modern cultures.